Bringing The Light Into A New Day:

African Centered Rites of Passage

By

Lathardus Goggins II

Saint Rest Publications
Akron, OH

Printed in the United States of America

Library of Congress Catalog Card Number: 98-090295
Goggins II, Lathardus
     Bringing the light into a new day: African centered
rites of passage/Lathardus Goggins II
     Includes notes and references (p. 125)
     1. African American Studies-Rites of Passage.
     2. Family/Parenting. 3. Anthropology-African
     American-Socialization. 4. Psychology-Cognitive
     Development 5. Education. I. Title
                              ISBN 0-9663972-0-7

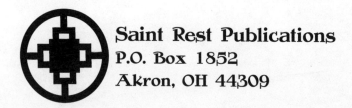

Saint Rest Publications
P.O. Box 1852
Akron, OH 44309

Acknowledgments
Asante Sana (Thank You)

All honor and praise to the Creator of us all, the original ancestor from whom all blessings, wisdom and power flows.

Hallelujah-Asante sana, Jesus for your saving grace and mercy.

Asante sana to the ancestors. It is their blood, work and prayers on which we stand.

Let us remember the people who sacrificed their lives and those who were killed during our struggle. Let us mourn the lost potential of the millions who perished during the middle passage, the thousands who died due to brutality of American oppression, and the daily slaughter by those whose minds are in the hands of the oppressor.

Asante sana to the community elders and scholars who have provided guidance and have reminded us of our "true" selves.

Asante sana to all those who provided wisdom, support and encouragement in the writing of this book: especially, Lathardus Goggins III, Dietra, Drs. Lathardus & Ellen O. Goggins, Venecia Clarke, Stephanie P. Toles, Dr. Kimetris Baltrip, Edwin & Kathy Baylock, Nathan & Yvonne Oliver, Dr. Ruth Z. Osborne, Sofornia Carr, Dr. Elnora Roane, Debra Wilcox, Paul Hill Jr., Mshindi Mkataa, Dr. Dianne Wright, Pastor Ronald J. Fowler, Emily-Diane Gunter, Dr. Myles Munroe, Dr. Mwalimu Shujaa, Darryl L. Mobley, Freedom Raynes Washington, Verona K. Williams-Chin, and Carolyn Hann.

Let us remember the unborn and persons new to the earth. Let all that we do lead them to knowledge of God, knowledge of authentic self and knowledge of their specific purposes.

Ashe!

Cover design and art work by Lathardus Goggins II and Mshindi Mkataa

Dedicated to:
> Douglas Sr. & Willice Goggins, Moses L. & Evangeline Osborne, and to their "great grands."

Contents

Emily-Diane Gunter, National Exec. Dir.,
Rites of Passage Youth Empowerment Programs of America
Author, **Superlearning 2000**

In today's environment, helping to turn the youth's energy focus is difficult, painstaking and unglamorous. It requires a long and serious commitment from the volunteer elders, the community, and the parents. The Rites of Passage Process also produces some of the most imaginative and successful juvenile delinquency, pregnancy and drug preventive reduction tactics we know. <u>Bringing The Light Into a New Day: African Centered Rites of Passage</u> offers a solid foundation for beginning a Rites of Passage Process.

Preventive measures make sure the youth never start down those roads of delinquency, pregnancy or drugs. Preventive measures help the youth to choose a positive life path. Through the Rites of Passage Process, the youth learn through EMPOWERMENT instead of through FEAR. This Program teaches teamwork, leadership, values and responsibility at an early age. The Rites of Passage process brings youth and elders together so the elders can pass on tradition, culture, history, and their special knowledge. The youth turn to delinquency, pregnancy and drugs because they lack self-esteem and a positive self-image. Therefore, it is important to improve the youth's sense of self-worth without specific reference to delinquency, pregnancy or drugs. This point is stressed in Goggins' first book, <u>African Centered Rites Of Passage and Education</u>, 1996.

One African proverb states, "It takes a village to raise a child." Parents are the children's first models for behavior and beliefs. Raising children is never easy, and raising them in poverty and in neighborhoods infested with crime and drugs, and in families with only one parent can be extremely difficult. The Rites of Passage Process provides these families with the village. The village is the volunteer elders from the community who facilitate the youth through challenges, experiential exercises and workshops.

The Rites Process will help decrease dropout rates, increase attendance at school, enhance grade point averages, enhance citizenship grades and increase college enrollment. In the war against juvenile delinquency and pregnancy, the real heroes are not those who use drugs, get pregnant, or get involved in crime and quit, but those who never get involved in the first place. This is the primary goal of prevention, to see to it that juveniles never start down a slippery slope of drug use that begins with "experimentation" but could culminate in dependency, and lead to crime and/ or pregnancy.

All children can learn no matter what the circumstances of their birth, or environment. Every parent and all adults must work as teachers to install in children an ethos of achievement. Every disadvantaged, underserved child responds best when expectations are high, not low, when goals are raised, not lowered. We must help every child develop their qualities of character and notions of right and wrong. We must help them obtain a since of self and a sense of purpose in their young lives. The Rites of Passage Process turns the youth onto themselves, their genius, their brilliance, their high values, their life, so they choose not to turn to drugs, delinquency, and pregnancy.

After parents, the school is probably the most influential on youth's lives. Schools are crushed under the burden of dropouts due to drugs, pregnancy, and delinquency. The Rites of Passage process is structured to sustain a village's interaction with its youth. The elders of the Rites of Passage assist the raising of the youth by intervening at the first sign of any involvement in drugs, pregnancy, and delinquency. The elders help the youth to realize their potential and give our youth the tools for today's decisions and tomorrow's success. The Rites of Passages used in America originated in Africa. The African Rites of Passage tradition passed down to us by our ancestors prescribes the eight basic elements:

(1)   the elders/facilitator of the program
(2)   the separation of the young women-the retreat
(3)   the preparation and use of the sacred place for the program
(4)   the release of emotional baggage, and old habits
(5)   the challenges
(6)   the transition to self-love and self-acceptance
(7)   the new awakenings, new beginnings
(8)   the celebration of joining the circle of adults

The African Rites tradition is an academic system of teaching through experiential exercises, pictures, systems, and forms. It is a process used to guide and nurture our youth. Each village/tribe customized this program depending on their youth's needs. The elders of the village knew it was necessary to define and transform destructive habits into new life habits for the youth.

In the African tradition, youth come into adulthood through the **passage on of knowledge and tradition**. Traditional African societies recognized the importance of guiding their youth successfully into adulthood. In these societies it was understood that with adulthood came responsibilities to oneself, family, community, and nation. Men and women were regarded as much more than just husbands, fathers, wives and mothers. The African societies initiated the youth into the culture and the heritage of their people through an academic and educational process called Rites of Passage. After the Rites, the youth was entrusted to uphold, teach, and preserve the heritage for the new generations yet to come.

In the African tradition, the youth must ask for the RITE (right) or permission OF PASSAGE (passing on) to a higher level of human social and educational development. After the youth have demonstrated competency in their academic and personal development during the rites program, permission for crossover or passage is granted by the elders in the community.

It is becoming an African American tradition for the elders of the community to come together for the purpose of helping our youth. The Rites of Passage Process can be tailored and designed to meet the needs and beliefs of its youth. This book was written with the belief that "**the most valuable asset our community has is our youth.**" It is necessary for our youth to move forward into the future as mentally, emotionally, intellectually, physically, and spiritually balanced community members.

Peace and Blessings,
Elder Emily-Diane Gunter

Preface

Paul Hill Jr., CEO/President, East End Neighborhood House
Founder, National Rites of Passage Institute-Cleveland, OH
Author, **Coming of Age: African American Male Rites of Passage**

The journey of discovery is not seeking new lands but seeing with new eyes. As we approach the new millennium and beyond, seeing with new eyes will be crucial to the quality of our existence. Bringing the Light Into a New Day: African Centered Rites of Passage is a foundational expansion of Goggins' first book, African Centered Rites of Passage and Education. The four chapters of this book provide a Christian-based blueprint for understanding and practicing African centered rites of passage.

"Light" as incorporated in the title of the book is used as a metaphor for opportunity, hope and wisdom. His book is predicated on the thesis that African centered rites of passage is the means for bringing the light or opportunity, energy, and wisdom into a much needed new day. His book suggests that we as African Americans are living in the most dangerous times since our presence in the Americas. The light that African centered rites of passage has the potential to provide, will enable us to see with new eyes. It will provide African Americans with a new way of thinking and doing.

African centered rites of passage will provide us with a new but old paradigm that enabled African ancestors and African ancestors born in America to deal with the absurd; and not succumb to the nihilistic threat of American and western existence.

Chapters one through four provide the superstructure and infrastructure for African centered rites of passage. Chapter one provides the foundation through a discussion of the philosophy and methods needed for cultural continuity in general, and African centered rites of passage in particular. Chapter two focuses on African cultural context and provides minimum principles (spirituality, harmony, movement, energy, affect, communalism, expressive individualism, oral tradition, and social time perspective) that recur as common themes among African people in the communities and families per ritual and ceremony throughout the diaspora.

Chapter three provides the reader with the existential scaffolding that is necessary for transformation through the rites of passage process, referencing examples of transformation that are Christian-based, historical, and experiential.

Whereas, chapters one through three discuss the concepts and components of African centered rites of passage; chapter four presents strategies and steps for the implementation of an African centered, family based, community linked rites of passage process. Insightful information is provided on ancestors, elders, code of conduct, life cycles, naming ceremony, learning circle activities and examples of lesson plans.

Bringing the Light Into a New Day: African Centered Rites of Passage is an important book in the evolving African centered rites of passage movement, and must be read by all students and practitioners of African centered rites of passage.

Paul Hill, Jr.

Introduction

Bringing the Light ...

In the title of this book, I use the metaphor "Bringing the light into a new day" to refer to the familiar quotes and statements about light and the coming of the dawn. Here are just a few:

Psalm 27:1 (NIV) - The Lord is my light and salvation....

Psalm 30:5 - ... weeping may remain for a night, but rejoicing comes in the morning. (NIV)

Matthew 5:14-16 - You are the light of the world. .... let your light shine before men, that they may see your good deeds and praise your Father in heaven.

John 8:12 (NIV) - .. I am the light of the world. Whoever follows me will never walk in darkness, but will have the light of life.

Nelson Mandela - Our deepest fear is not that we are inadequate. Our deepest fear is that we are powerful beyond measure. It is our Light, not our Darkness, that most frightens us.

Martin L. King Jr. - Light has come into the world, and every man must decide whether he will walk in the light of altruism or the darkness of destructive selfishness.

Mahatma Gandhi - In the attitude of silence, the soul finds the path in a clearer light, and what is elusive and deceptive resolves itself into crystal clearness. Our life is a long and arduous quest after Truth.

Joni E. Tada - Faith in small things has repercussions that ripple all the way out. In a huge, dark room a little match can light up the place.

Chinese Proverb - Better to light a candle than to curse the darkness.

Light is used to represent opportunity, hope and wisdom. Those sayings which suggest we must wait for the morning imply we also must have faith or the dawn will not come, and thus all hope is gone. I suggest that we must be active participants in the creation and management of this "light," if we are to benefit from it.

From the physical world, we see a parallel principle: Each day the sun provides the earth with enough energy to maintain life; each night the energy of yesterday must be used until the dawn. If not, all would freeze and die during the night. The light of each day is new to that day; however, its source is as old as the solar system (about 4.5 billion years). Each day is a dynamic interaction of the past being applied to the future. How foolish would it be for people on Earth to deny the existence of our sun, and try to harness the energy of a distant star?

African American families and communities must bring the light (opportunity, energy, wisdom) into the new day. Our light is our heritage, a dynamic interaction of the past and future creating new solutions for our present. If we do not bring this light into the new day, then we doom ourselves: at worst, to die during the night; at best, to be cast in the faint light of someone else's star, unable to see our own potential. Let us remember the words of Marcus Garvey:

Chance has never yet satisfied the hope of a suffering people. Action, self-reliance, the vision of self and the future have been the only means by which the oppressed have seen and realized the light of their own freedom.

To bring the light is to invoke sankofa: to go back and fetch what has worked. Here the implication is to reflect, and study the past, future, and present in order to create needed solutions (Tedla, 1996). Please be careful to note, sankofa is not just repeating old ways of doing things. Rather, sankofa is an examination of the future and the past, then applying only those things from the past in the present that will help create the desired future.

It seems that too many people of African descent, particularly in the United States, are inadequately equipped to create successful positive solutions for their lives. The lack of collective cultural wisdom provides the impetus for trying to understand oneself based upon others' values and philosophies, which often leads to self confusion, doubt, stagnation and oppression. This results in a pathological existence, one in which individuals use values and philosophies meant to dehumanize them in order to "try" to maximize their human existence. Such is the case for many African Americans, who try to become "mainstream" by using values and philosophies which were used to separate them from the mainstream. The resulting pathologies (acting white, racelessness, acceptance, and oppositional culture) can be seen in African American communities.

I use the terms black, Black and African American to discuss the distinctions between people of African descent. There have been many terms "we" have used to refer to ourselves. The transition from Colored to African or African American is reflective of the redefining of people of African descent in the United States. For this discussion, the term of choice is "African American" to refer to the ethnic group. Black (capitalized) refers to "state of mind," while black denotes race (Biko, 1997).

Those blacks employing the "acting white" strategy deny their African heritage in order to try to "become" white. One of the tragic flaws of this thinking is the assumption of

American mainstream's willingness to accept them, if they look and act white enough. Typically, these blacks have become tokens of the "redeeming" characteristics of European supremacy or they become spectacles of absurdity. The paradox of this strategy is that to gain one's freedom, one must justify his/her own oppression.

Blacks (black) who realize that they can not become white, yet still see the "need" to shun their African heritage often use a racelessness strategy. Here the objective is to be non threatening by being "un-Black." With basic premise being that Black is detrimental, being un-Black (culture neutral) will allow others to accept them. Acceptance or "Uncle Tomming" is a strategy by which one tries to gain favor from the mainstream by maximizing the docile stereotypes of African Americans.

The aforementioned strategies are all meant to gain favor from the dominant culture. To the contrary, those who use oppositional culture strategy are trying to reject the dominant culture. The objective is to be Black by purging themselves of what is perceived to be white or European. Oppositional culture strategy gives the perception of taking control. However, the truth is those who employ this strategy use mainstream values and philosophies to justify their existence as much as anyone using the acting white, racelessness or acceptance strategies. In order to be "anti-white," one's first reference point is "what is white." Considering the vast majority of African Americans have been schooled in racist dominated culture institutions, many of those who employ the oppositional culture strategy have false perceptions of white supremacy. Thus, by purging out what is perceived to be white, one is often left with inferior qualities. The apparent questions are, "What strategy should be used?", and "How can the light be brought?" The answer: African Centered Rites of Passage!

My discussion about rites of passage will be latent with the group values, philosophies and experiences that affected/effected/infected my life. As a reader, it is important to understand this book represents my interpretations. It is my intention to present the following information in a scholarly, truthful, and understandable manner. However, the content will not be "totally objective," as if research can ever be totally without assumptions and bias. Therefore, it is necessary to frame my discussion in order for you, the reader, to better consciously interpret and evaluate this work.

There are two primary motivations for my discussions on African centered rites of passage. One is a response to Steve Biko's classic statement, "The greatest weapon in the hands of the oppressor are the minds of the oppressed." The second is to seek and articulate an understanding of why "certain" people develop a self-consciousness beyond their "apparent circumstances" and achieve "success."

I am writing from an African centered view, which requires moral and spiritual code. I will use Christianity. Please note that I clearly distinguish Christianity (the philosophies and teachings of Jesus) from "the white man's religion" (religious traditions based on the grossly distorted teachings of Jesus in order to unjustly perpetuate false concepts of White European male supremacy). I have experienced the rites of passage process as an initiate, facilitator, and scholar. I will draw upon all of these for this discussion of African centered rites of passage. Though much of the literature on rites of passage and my experiences as an initiate are male oriented, it is my intention to discuss the African centered family based, community linked rites of passage process (rites) in an inclusive manner as possible.

The purpose of this book is to discuss thoroughly: the purpose and function of rites; the structure and process of rites; the components of rites; the transforming power of rites; and strategies, rituals, ceremonies, activities that construct rites process. It should be noted that this is not a "how to" book; rather, it is a book meant to help the reader to know "how to how to." It is my intention to provide a guide to understanding "family based, community linked," African centered rites of passage. This follows the logic that if we all have been created for a unique purpose, then our development will also be unique. However, at the same time, we are not created to be self serving. We are created to serve others, thus community linked. It is impractical and detrimental to provide a "prepackage predetermined rites of passage."

Bringing The Light Into A New Day is meant to provide a "black print" or scaffolding by which you can construct a rites of passage process that is consistent with African heritage and your family tradition, while connecting the initiates (see note 1) to their community.

The Purpose and Function of African Centered Rites of Passage

ESE NE KETER EMA
(Teeth and Tongue)

No child is born with its teeth.
We improve and advance.

The primary purpose of the rites of passage process is to transfer the collective "cultural wisdom" of a people to members of the group. To transfer their collective wisdom, a coherent society will use rituals and ceremonies to provide metaphors for the philosophies and values which shape that society. Therefore a heathy society creates structures by which members can successfully come to know purpose and meaning for their lives. These structures are typically arranged to correspond with stages of life or states of consciousness as defined by the society. It is this combination of rituals, ceremonies and the corresponding conceptual structures which form the rites of passage process.

In many "modern" societies the rites of passage process has been replaced with a formal education system. Nonetheless, the rites of passage process is universal to the human condition. Regardless of where humans are, there will be rites of passage. What changes are the deliberateness and consciousness of the values and philosophies being transferred. By transferring collective wisdom, a society ensures its existence and development. The conscious transferring of collective cultural wisdom (heritage) provides a base for developing new ideas, self determination, and historical continuity, while encouraging extended family (fictive kinship) bonds and communal responsibilities. Conversely, a society that does not consciously transfer collective cultural wisdom relegates each generation to "invent" old ideas, and will ultimately lead to the death and destructions of that society. Thus, the loss or "heathenizing" of the rites process has been one of the most devastating legacies of slavery and colonialism of African people.

The methods and philosophies used to disrupt the cultural continuity of a people have been discussed by various scholars (see note 2 and Appendix 1). Some of the methods and philosophies used in the "New World" to oppress blacks were and continue to be: breaking family and fictive kinship bonds, brutal control over cultural symbols, and validating those who abandon personal and cultural integrity for the sake of white European male supremacy. Fundamentally, in order to oppress a group of people effectively over long periods of time, an oppressor must sever sankofa - the historical continuity achieved by transferring collective cultural wisdom.

The relevant literature strongly asserts that culture is a learned activity. Cultural values and ethos are transmitted through the evaluation of experiences - a primarily cognitive process. However, where the issues of the black race are concerned, it seems many people believe that culture is a function of race, a primarily genetic process. Unfortunately, many in the African American community have also adopted this belief. A belief that race equals culture is a product of a racist and oppressive system (Maquet, 1967/1972). As Freire (1970) stated, the projection of absolute ignorance onto the oppressed is a tendency of the oppressor. In the United States, the mainstream used race as justification for oppression. Being black (genetic) is the reason for ignorance. Ignorance (cognitive) is the reason for deficient culture (performance).

Many African Americans have taken issue with the Race/Genetic-> Ignorance/Cognitive -> Culture/Performance assumption. To do so, African American scholars and leaders have attacked the assumption of ignorance and deficiency, by providing examples to the contrary. However, many have accepted the connection between race and culture. Consequently, genetic characteristics have often been used as criteria to determine culture. Thick lips and nose, "tightly curled" hair, "big" butt, and dark skin have often been used as determinants for African self consciousness. Of course, how one values such characteristics <u>may</u> reflect frame of reference, but having such characteristics does not equate to African centered frame of reference. Culture should be seen as a deliberate and conscious act, one demanding a conscious and deliberate transmission to the next generation (Hill, 1987; Kunjufu, 1985; Perkins, 1986; Some, 1994).

Imagine if students simply went to school until they had enough, with no test or chance to discuss what they learned with knowledgeable people. Students receive no evaluation of their skills, nor do they have any constructed opportunities to practice what they have learned. Students could sit in on classes, but have no required classes. No graduation. Just at the end of the day someone tells you, "You're done; don't come back." Sounds crazy? How much less ludicrous is it to bestow adulthood or eldership on someone just because he or she wandered around long enough?

By providing African centered rites of passage to African descendants throughout the diaspora, the African community ensures its existence and that individuals throughout the African community will better understand what it is to be a member of the African community. The culturally and spiritually based rites of passage process is not a panacea for life's problems, just as exercising and eating "right" do not guarantee that a person will not have a heart attack or other medical conditions. However, persons who have exercised are better prepared to deal with a medical condition than if they had not exercised. Likewise, a person who has entered a cultural-spiritually based rites of passages is better prepared to deal with life than someone who has not.

The proverb, "It is better to raise a child than to fix a man," provides some insight into when one should enter the rites process. It confirms that proactive conscious development, such as cultural-spiritually based rites of passage, is something with which one should start life. Many development theorists support the notion that personality, thinking patterns/cognitive schemes, and consciousness development start very early in life (Young, 1996). According to Freud's (1933) Psychoanalytic Theory of human development, one's basic personality is set by age five. Theorist Erikson (1982) has put forth a Psychosocial Theory of development, based on Freud (Shaffer, 1993), that maintains there are eight stages of development. Each stage has a conflict or crisis that must be resolved before passing onto the next stage of life. However, if these crises are not resolved, then the individual will eventually lose the ability to adapt to society. Thus, it is necessary to resolve childhood before adolescence and adulthood. Even behaviorists, such as B. F. Skinner (1953), suggest that the habits formed during childhood are powerful predictors of what is possible in adulthood. Cognitive development theorists focus their attention on the development of thinking patterns. Piaget (1954) suggests there are four stages of development through which children must progress: sensorimotor, preoperational, concrete operational, and formal operational. One cannot reach the final stage of cognitive development without successfully completing the previous stages.

Most recently, research on the development of the brain has provided new awareness to the importance of early proactive conscious development. Researchers have found that there are "windows of opportunities" in which certain development should (and in some cases must) take place. Some windows close as early as age two. The research suggests that the first ten years of life are critical. Once past this stage, "hard wiring" connections between cells and parts of the brain no longer take place; only those connections that have been "substantially" used will be maintained, while unused connections fade away. What I find interesting is that theories of human development from psychology, biology, and anthropology point to the transition to adulthood around age thirteen, emphasizing the importance and enduring effect of development of "self" (see note 3) in childhood to the rest of a person's life.

The African centered rites of passage process is not a single ceremony or a program a child goes through at age thirteen, but a process which takes the individual from birth to ancestry - from the Creator to the Creator. Dr. Anthony Mensah defines rites of passage as:

> ... those structures, rituals and ceremonies by which age-class members or individuals in a group successfully come to know who they are and what they are about - the purpose and meaning for their existence, as they proceed from one clearly defined state of existence to the next state or passage in their lives.

African centered rites of passage is a process which an individual enters. It is meant to be a vehicle for self-conscious development. Each ritual and ceremony is a marker, collectively a map to understanding one's purpose - the why to which the Creator has created. Depending on the traditions and philosophies of the group, each transition through various stages of life would be marked differently. However, each would be marked. Here again the proverbs speak to us: "If you do not know where you are going, any direction will do." The proverb suggests that not only should development be a deliberate act, but also that proper development starts with the end in mind. Otherwise, any behavior is acceptable and any idea has merit. Therefore, life has no meaning or focus. There is no code of conduct based in cultural heritage, and no defense against the racist philosophies prevalent in the American system.

These are symptoms of what Dr. Francine Childs

(1997) calls "CAIDS" (Culturally Acquired Immunity Deficiency Syndrome). She is obviously drawing a parallel with AIDS; a disease caused when a harmful foreign virus infects a host. The virus attacks and weakens the immune system. The immune system is weakened to the point where "opportunistic" viruses, bacteria and fungi cause deadly sickness and the body slowly rots away. Opportunistic denotes those viruses, bacteria and fungi that are not a threat to a healthy system, only to bodies with weakened defenses. Also, AIDS is a social disease. It is passed from host to host through sharing body fluids (experiences which should give life).

Likewise, a person suffering from CAIDS is infected with racist philosophies. These philosophies have attacked and weakened the host's mind until he or she is incapable of coping with conditions that a "healthy" person could. Though few CAIDS victims die as a direct result of a racist act, CAIDS causes victims to make deadly decisions. Examples include killing one's consciousness and potential by underdeveloping and misusing talents by undervaluing self; one's mission (purpose) in life; one's responsibility to the Creator, family and community; and by mimicking "others" and adopting others' interpretations of one's existence. In this state of confusion, victims suffering from CAIDS often infect those to whom they should be giving life, thereby ensuring the sickness is passed throughout a community and from generation to generation. Individuals and communities suffering from CAIDS are left to whims of "opportunistic" philosophies and systems of oppression, which depend upon the oppressed to participate in their oppression.

In the United States, people of African descent suffering from CAIDS do not have a strong connection to African cultural heritage. Subsequently, a person does not have the basic tenants necessary to form a philosophical construct that places him/herself and his/her purpose at the center, allowing him/her to make meaningful decisions. The Bible warns "without a vision, the people will perish." Likewise, without a vision of or understanding about his/ her life purpose, a person will lose his or her energy, spirit, and mind (Frankl, 1962).

This also implies that it is dangerous to enter a rites of passage process with no understanding of what is the intended outcome. Ronald Johnson (1996) identifies at least ten different "kinds" of rites of passage:

1. Personal - self consciousness and concept
2. Emotional - manage emotion, code of conduct
3. Mental - intellect
4. Physical/Health - maturation and fitness
5. Political - understanding systems of power
6. Social - understanding one's place within the social structure
7. Historical Competency - knowing the family and cultural history
8. Cultural - nuance and style
9. Economic - self supportive
10. Spiritual - relationship with God

Each of these rites of passage process is meant to develop a particular aspect of the "self." Therefore, the intended outcome demands specific content. In other words, "College begins in kindergarten" (Wright, 1997) and adulthood starts in childhood. It is this continuity between stages of life which makes rites of passage so powerful.

To use a sport analogy, it is the concept of "momentum" when a team builds upon previous moments to elevate their play. Basketball often provides excellent examples. Momentum is when a dunk, steal, a good play sparks the team to a series of good plays to the extent that it seems they can do "no wrong." Each moment transfers to the next moment energy and confidence to a point that it becomes overwhelming, not only for the opponent, but for the team itself. Members of the team anticipate, respond and think at levels not normally reached. When individuals reach this level of play, it is often described as "being in a zone." In this situation, the opponent will try to break the continuity of the moments by calling time out or fouling. The essence of this analogy is also true for a group of people.

When a group of people builds upon the work and understandings of previous members, the group experiences momentum. Take scientists and inventors, specifically the Wright brothers, for example. They have been recognized as the first to have "documented" mechanical flight. They used available technology to create the new technology, one of which was the concept of a self-lubricating engine, pioneered by Elijah McCoy. Another example, Alexander G. Bell's telephone, was a single line between two receivers. However, by using the innovations developed by Grandville T. Woods, telephones were networked together and, eventually, computers too, thus the internet. How productive can a scientist be if he or she had to invent every concept and technology used? It is because of historical and collective continuity, being able to access the understandings of other members that a Wright flyer and the space shuttle can exist just 70 years apart. What is true for scientists, as a group, is true for other groups.

A society, family and/or individual that is connected to the understandings of previous members will experience momentum. Each experience draws upon the collective wisdom of past experiences to propel a society, family and/ or individual into the future. This is the essence of sankofa. We also see this same concept in Proverbs 13:22, "A good man leaves an inheritance to his children's children." If each generation has to build a "nest egg," when will it hatch? Please note the inheritance is not just material things, but includes understanding, wisdom, safety - essentially, the means to be productive.

Sankofa tells us to reach higher levels of existence, we must build upon the collective wisdom of African people. It also implies that without reflecting on the collective wisdom, a society, family and/or individual is weak or stagnant. Thus, collective wisdom must be accessible and transmitted.

Ten Basic Assumptions
(adopted in part from Dr. Anthony Mensah)

Not only is African centered, family based, community linked rites of passage a method for transmitting collective cultural wisdom, it is a necessary response to beliefs about the relationship between the Creator and the development of authentic self.

The Creator does not create for failure. This is a recognition that if God creates something, then it is created for a specific purpose and that purpose is not to fail.

All humans are one with the Cosmos (the Creator and creation). This stems from the understanding that all things are connected to one another, both physically and spiritually. Whether you subscribe to evolution (science), creation (spiritual) or both (see note 4), it is an undeniable fact. Specifically, let us examine humans. According to the theories of evolution, all life is connected. The great diversity of life forms on Earth has a common ancestor, and that ancestor was a by-product from the materials (chemicals and compounds) that formed the Earth. The Earth was formed from elements of the universe. Also, mathematically all things are connected through gravity. Each thing in the universe has a direct gravitational pull on every other thing in the universe (see note 5).

The theory of creation states that God created man from the dust of the Earth. God made the human body from the materials already in the universe. Not only do humans share common materials with the universe, we share the Creator. When an artist creates, each creation is an expression of the artist. The same is true for the universe (the creation). Each aspect of the universe is tied together by the Creator and expresses some characteristic of the Creator. Consequently, we must recognize that each person is part of the cosmic whole. Therefore, we must seek to understand our place and responsibilities in the Cosmos.

Every person has the capacity to succeed. Because the Creator does not design for failure, all people have within them the potential to fulfill successfully their purpose.

We are born with a driving intent to express the capacity to succeed. Not only is every person born with the capacity to succeed, but also has within him or her a "nagging" need to be successful.

When the intent of the Creator is not met with appropriate content, a person's potential for success is ruined. This is the recognition that a person may be born to succeed and has the need to succeed; however, without proper preparation ability to succeed is lost. This also implies that "proper" is relative. What is proper content for one may not be proper for another. Therefore, it is imperative that those who provide the preparation are in tune with the Creator to discern the specific intent of an initiate.

Inappropriate content brings reaction, and not intellectual growth, and the child's ability to interact (use his or her intelligence) falls increasingly behind. Thus, the further one's intelligence falls behind, the more energy must go into compensation. This is an understanding that without proper preparation a child will not have the mental tools to be creative, proactive, productive and "fit" into the community. Without such preparation, "anything" can cause a child to respond. The child has no discipline or patience. And, the longer the child is left in this state, the more energy, time, money, and resources will have to be spent to correct the damages.

With the infusion of inappropriate content, the young person's intelligence is still out there in the previous passage, trying to make functional [sense] the intent of the Creator. Rites of passage helps a person move successfully into the next stage and corresponding responsibilities. Without rites (proper content and preparation) a person will move through life physically with a consciousness stuck at the last stage he or she could complete successfully. For example, many of us know 30 or 40 year old teenagers. These are people trying to live a 30-40 year old's existence with a mentality of a teenager, playing teenage games in an adult world. This is not to suggest that one should grow "old" in the negative way that mainstream society implies. Old or eldership does not mean feebleness or uselessness. However, as the Apostle Paul implies in I Corinthians 13:11, "When I was a child, I talked like a child, I thought like a child, I reasoned like a child. When I became a man, I put childish ways behind me." With proper preparation elders are griots, wisdom keepers, teachers and leaders in families and the community.

He who does not cultivate his field will die of hunger. This proverb conveys the understanding that a community that does not nurture its children will eventually die. Everything that the community needs to grow is potentially in its children. The next doctor, entrepreneur, artist, teacher, you name it... whatever the community needs will be found in its children.

Rites of Passage in the child's education provides a meaningful response to the intent. The success of the Creator's plan hinges directly on the person (infant, child, adolescent, or adult) being provided with content proper for

the intent of that person. This logic stems directly from the implications of the aforementioned assumptions. If the Creator creates each person to fulfill his or her purpose successfully and the Creator instills within each person the "drive" to express his or her purpose; if one must be prepared to express his or her purpose; and if the Creator's intent for a person is meant to "nourish" a community and eventually the Cosmos, then a process where people come to know and understand their unique purpose (talent, gift, mission, genius) is necessary. Not to provide such a process is ultimately detrimental to the community. Consequently, a malnourished community must spend its social energy and capital fixing the damages and insanity of its members, particularly the youth. In fact, not to provide such a process is to be in direct opposition to the Creator and out of rhythm with the Cosmos (Evans, 1993).

Also, this belief implies that education is a divine endeavor, a partnership between the individual, family, community and the Creator. Proper education provides the foundation to examine the world critically. It fosters intellectual growth by equipping a child with experiences and knowledge that help in the organizing and development of concepts. These concepts become the tenants and tools necessary to seek, understand, and strategize to fulfill each person's purpose.

All persons who experience this type of education will benefit from it. This is an affirmation that if the family and community have provided an educational process by which a person can learn to align him or her self with the intent of the Creator, then "good" happens. The Cosmos moves on your behalf: "If God be for you, who can stand against you?" (Romans 8:31).

Meaning Making, Consciousness, Context

If the purpose of the African centered rites of passage process is to be a vehicle for conscious self development by transferring collective cultural wisdom, then the function of rites is to provide a context in which active "meaning making" can take place by a conscious being. To understand the function of rites, we must examine three concepts: "active meaning making," "conscious being," and "context."

Active meaning making is the process by which a person assigns significance and understanding to symbols, ideas and experiences. In short, active meaning making is active learning. Active denotes a person who is purposefully engaged in meaning making, a person who takes responsibility for learning and applies "self" to an experience. To meaning make actively is to be a critical thinker - not cynical or pessimistic, but seeking truth, understanding and integrity.

Critical thinking requires a person to sort fact from fiction, filter emotions, focus on solutions, prioritize wants, responsibilities and needs, reflect on experiences, and select credible resources. A person engaged in active meaning making is better able to:

1. Resist oppression and manipulation
2. Discern the connection between symbols, experiences and concepts
3. Overcome confusion
4. Manage the complexities of life

It is this search for truth, understanding and integrity which tends to entice the need for self examination, an imperative for self consciousness.

Consciousness is one of those vague terms we often

use, which tend to mean different things to different people. I will use another sport analogy to illustrate my definition of consciousness. When an athlete's consciousness is being examined, he or she is evaluated on his or her strength, balance, and response to the following questions: Where are you? What's your name? How many fingers do you see? Can you follow an object with your eyes? How do you feel/Can you protect yourself? Do you want to continue? I suggest to you that a conscious person could:

1. Control oneself in order to garner enough strength for the task at hand.
2. Control one's actions to move in sync with one's intentions.
3. Articulate and know who one is, which also implies an understanding of whose one is, to whom one is accountable, and for what one will be held accountable (purpose).
4. Articulate a clear vision of oneself and one's environment.
5. Accurately assess one's position as it relates to executing purpose.
6. Assess one's attributes and determine one's effectiveness in executing one's purpose, through self reflection (which also implies a person can analyze the obstacles and challenges to be faced).
7. Amass the willpower to execute purpose.

It should also be noted that consciousness is not a static state, but dynamic awareness of becoming. One does not simply become "aware" and then no longer need to reflect and examine one's self and environment. Awareness and active meaning making are continuous. Now the question is: How does one become conscious?

Various Nigrescence (Black Identity Development) models have maintained there are five stages to Black consciousness: 1) Pre-encounter, 2) Encounter, 3) Immersion-Emersion, 4) Internalization, and 5)

Internalization-Commitment. These models suggest that Black identity or African self consciousness is a function of some event in which one can no longer deny one's "Blackness." As often implied, the event is traumatic and negative in nature: "...having a rug pulled from under you" (Cross, Parham, & Helms, 1991). Next, this person immerses his/her self into a search for African identity. The Nigrescence models also state that a person in this stage of consciousness will tend to develop a counter culture or militant reference to mainstream. The fourth and fifth stages of consciousness are Internalization and Internalization-Commitment, respectively. Internalization is the stage where the new identity is internalized. This indicates a resolution between the old and new self. This is also the stage where one's reference center moves from responding to mainstream to being African. Internalization-Commitment is the stage where a person finds and becomes committed to his or her life's purpose.

What sparks the development of African self consciousness? Simply the need to "be." Some experience forces one to consider the question articulated by Asa Hilliard III: "To be African or not to be?" Hilliard is not simply asking to be African or not to be African, but to accept one's African heritage or cease to exist, to lose one's consciousness and meaning.

I would argue that the nature of the encounter has a major effect/affect on the development of consciousness. As most often described, the development of African self consciousness is reactive, not proactive. As aforementioned, to develop a sense of self in opposition to something is to be centered by that something. Therefore, few are able to move into Internalization and Internalization-Commitment. However, when families, churches, and community organizations provide African centered rites of passage as an essential part of the healthy development of a person, there is no old self to reconcile. The African centered rites of passage process provides a proactive and positive context to "encounter" the need for African self consciousness.

Context refers to the surrounding factors which support a particular event, concept or process. There is a context which sustains the "rites" process and a context created by the process. Anthony Mensah (in MECCA, n.d) describes one group of factors which aids in the rites process as the matrix, which consists of energy, potential and safety.

Energy represents the efforts of the Creator, the initiate, ancestors, parents, family and community. Potential is the gifts, talents and purposes placed within the initiate (the intent of the Creator), and their development. The further one develops his or her talents, the greater the potential. However, the opposite is also true. The longer a talent is undeveloped, the greater the decrease in potential (see note 6). Safety is the place where the enemy and danger do not reach. For example, the womb provides the optimal conditions for the baby to grow and develop, protected from the outside world. However, at some point in the development, it becomes necessary to enter the world. If proper development has taken place, the baby would have developed some ability (realized potential) to aid in its survival. As parents, we should provide protection from those things that are still a threat: from others who would do harm (physical, emotional, intellectual), weather and general dangers (baby proofing the house). As the child grows, we introduce and provide opportunities for the baby to take challenges until what once was a danger is no longer so.

Also, a part of creating safety is identifying who are friends, allies and enemies. Friends are those who will work directly and regularly with the initiates to facilitate fulfilling the initiates' intent. Allies are people and organizations that may work with parents, family and community to meet the needs of the initiates, but do not work directly or regularly with the initiates. Enemies are simply anything that would deter the initiates from fulfilling their specific intent.

Let us not forget where we are. We are strangers in a strange land. For 246 (1619 - 1865) of the 379 (1619 - 1998) years (64.9%), the prevailing status or legal definition of African people by American society was one of property. Also, of these 379 years, people of African descent have had the protected right to vote (the right to make decisions about policy and resources) for only 41 years (1870 - 1877 and 1964 - 1998; 10.8%). Therefore, for 89% of the African presence in "American" society, the African American was legally marginalized and relegated to second class status. Though laws have changed and have been reinterpreted, many systems of oppression were left intact and are still operating today. It is simply foolish to think that the American society is no longer oppressive and racist.

The Apostle Paul urges the Ephesians to put on the full armor of God (Ephesians 6:11). The armor creates a safe place in the midst of those who would do harm. The function of African centered, family based, community linked rites of passage is to ensure a person finds and knows how to use the armor and the weapons formed for his or her specific mission, such as having the ability to turn stumbling blocks into stepping stones - reinterpreting information.

Culture provides the essential mental tools for interpretation. According to Vygotsky (1962), humans cognitively function at two levels: lower and higher. Lower cognitive functions include reactive attention, associate memory, and sensory motor thought. Vygotsky believes these are innate biological functions. Higher cognitive functioning consists of the maintenance and development of cultural tools/heritage or collective cultural wisdom. Generally, these mental tools fit into at least one of four categories: the ability to focus attention, deliberate memory, purpose and symbolic thought. For Vygotsky, the only method to reach high level thinking is in cohort with another (peer, teacher, parent). Vygotsky contends that a student can learn a certain amount of information on his/her own, and there is an amount of information that can be learned with the assistance of a teacher. What the student learns without help represents the lower end of the zone of proximal development (ZPD). The ZPD is the gap between what students can learn on their own and what students can learn with help. Vygotsky argues that learning is socio-cultural specific, maintaining that the social context has an influence on how and what we think.

Social learning theorist Albert Bandura (1977, 1986) supports the use of symbols as one of the cognitive factors which influence learning. It is through symbols that one will translate observations into internal models which can guide future actions and can be used to formulate possible courses of action before actual performance (P540 Bandura Group, 1996).

In my first book, <u>African Centered Rites of Passage and Education</u>, I represented this process in the Information Transformation Model

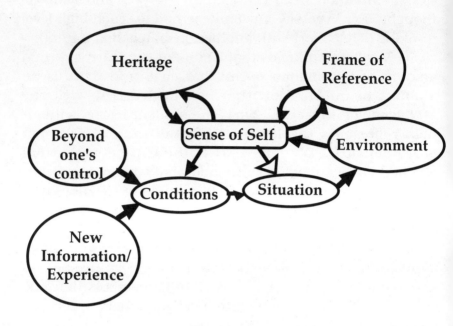

Frame of reference/World view is the philosophical conceptual framework used for seeing reality and understanding order. This includes an individual's concept of the relationships between self, nature and society.

Heritage refers to the set of techniques; strategies and traditions (collective wisdom) developed to solve problems of existence. Heritage is based upon the contributions of ancestors, elders and those in the current generation. Heritage, as it is defined here, is not a static heirloom simply passed from one generation to the next, but a dynamic interaction of antiquity and the present. This definition also implies that there is a collective and specific nature to heritage. There is a common heritage shared by a group of people. However, there are specific traits more prevalent within certain subgroups, such as a family.

Conditions are the existing circumstances which happen for reasons: 1) beyond the control of the individual,

2) new information/experiences or 3) created or influenced by the individual.

Situation is one's status in regard to conditions. Status is contingent upon one's evaluation of the circumstances. Evaluation is a function of the self (Rogers, 1956). Thus, for this discussion, situation is defined as the manifestation of the self through the application of values and ethos on a particular set of conditions.

Environment is the natural, social and cultural situations that affect development of self. Each new experience has within it both obvious and hidden values and meanings. Access to African cultural heritage allows people of African descent to evaluate and reinterpret experiences with the understanding of the ancestors and elders, thereby creating meanings and solutions consistent with (not necessarily the same as) the collective cultural wisdom. Without the ability to evaluate and reinterpret an experience, the values and meanings latent in that experience will become a part of the environment unchecked and unexamined. Once infecting a person's environment, the values and meanings will affect the development of self, which in turn will effect one's frame of reference, how one sees or does not see the world (CAIDS).

When the values and meanings that have infected and affected self development are based in white European males' superiority, a frame of reference develops which allows two people of African heritage to refer to one another as nigger (nigga) as common vernacular and see nothing wrong with it. This frame of reference will allow a pastor to hang a picture of a blond, blue-eyed Jesus, and not question the picture's validity, nor question what the image is doing to the minds (self) of the parishioners (see note 7). Youth will accept "mainstream" perceptions of their capabilities and avoid education for the sake of sports (see note 8). Essentially, these people are pathologically confused about their life's intent and responsibilities.

For African Americans, African centered rites of passage transfers the collective cultural wisdom, which contains the basic tenets for forming authentic self. These tenets include: 1) historical continuity, 2) development of meaning and purpose in one's life, 3) the ability to transform and interpret information (active meaning making), 4) community and parental expectations for development and maintenance of the society, and 5) development of fictive kinship bonds among members of the community. This person is more clearly able to discern how the Creator has worked through his or her family and one's own experiences to manifest intent for one's life.

For a person who has a strong sense of self that has been nurtured and supported by community, heritage and authentic expectations, his or her sense of self goes beyond a particular situation. For example, a student can enter a classroom or a set of conditions, be challenged at best or oppressed at worst, and deal with the circumstances at hand and not have his or her self efficacy (see note 9) crushed or determined by that moment. This becomes a situation that an individual goes through, not one by which the individual is defined. Instead, the individual learns how to define the situation.

The African centered rites of passage process provides a context which nurtures the linkage to heritage, therefore allowing a person to access collective wisdom when evaluating experience; this in turn, provides guides for interpreting information and developing strategies for fulfilling his or her mission (intent) in life. (Thus, the process promotes a person's positive self-efficacy, his or her sense of competence.) These are ultimately the purpose and functions of African centered rites of passage process.

The Structure and Process of African Centered Rites of Passage

MFRAMA-DAN
(Wind House)

A house built to stand
windy and treacherous conditions

There are some basic concepts that must be understood and components in place in order to construct and implement an African centered, family based, community linked rites of passage. The two "most" basic concepts are African cultural context and family traditions.

Perhaps Wade Nobles provided the best description of culture when he stated, "Culture is to humans as water is to fish." This statement points out that a person that is abruptly removed from his or her culture is like a fish out of water - suffocating, panic stricken, and unable to do what a fish does best. Not only does a fish need to be in water to be a fish effectively, but depending on the historical developments, certain fish need certain water conditions to flourish. For humans, culture is the median in which all activity takes place, and determines how an activity takes place. It is also true that groups of people have unique experiences which have shaped their symbols and meanings. These symbols and meanings have in turn influenced the way the group practices its activities. So in order for a person to maximize his or her potential, there must be synchronization between that person's particular cultural heritage and the activities in which he or she engages. This is not to suggest that we cannot and do not learn from other cultures. However, the new information and activities are best learned when they are interpreted through cultural filters (Biko, 1978; Irvine, 1991; Shade, 1989; Vygotsky, 1962). Cultural heritage provides the lenses by which we view and the foundation on which we interpret the world. Thus, learning cannot be separate from the social/cultural context of the learner. Consequently, culture is fundamental to the rites of passage process.

Therefore, African centered rites of passage must be consistent with the symbols and meanings developed by the philosophies of African people and cultures. Again, it should be noted that Africa is a diverse continent. Yet, despite the diversity among African people and their respective cultures, there are common themes.

African Cultural Context

According to Boykin (1986), traditional West African culture is centered around: 1) Spirituality, 2) Harmony, 3) Movement, 4) Energy, 5) Affect, 6) Communalism, 7) Expressive Individualism, 8) Oral Tradition, and 9) Social Time Perspective. Boykin's observations are consistent with research by Ani (1994), Asante (1987), Karenga (1994), Maquet (1967/1972), and Patton (1993).

Spirituality is an understanding that there is a creative life force which connects all phenomena and entities in the creation one to another. This understanding stems from a belief that there is a spirit realm which interacts with the natural. Spirituality is also a recognition that there are agendas, missions, purposes that the spirits are trying to fulfill in the natural world. And since humans are a part of both the natural and spirit worlds, then each person has a mission to fulfill. Simultaneously, one must choose which spirits to align him or herself and guard against being manipulated against one's purpose.

Harmony is a notion that seeks to allow all entities to coexist in order for each to maximize its purpose. This is not to say there are no "rights and wrongs" or absolutes. However, the emphasis is "both/and" and peace, rather than the Eurocentric tendency toward "either/or" and domination. The belief in harmony is the basis for the concepts of balance and rhythm in African cultures.

Balance between what is supernatural and natural, male and female, individual and village, old and new, and between the ancestors, elders, adults, children, and those not yet born. *(Please notice that I use supernatural and natural and not supernatural vs. natural - which is Eurocentric).* The concept of balance encourages one to find one's "proper" place and responsibilities in the Cosmos. Chaos is a function of persons not fulfilling their proper intent (see note 10). Therefore, there is emphasis on finding life's purpose and rituals which seek to foster acceptance and fulfillment of responsibilities.

Rhythm is more than just a musical concept. It is a recognition that certain things happen at particular times for a specific duration in synchronization with other phenomena. It is an understanding that it is not only important to find purpose and meaning in one's life, but it is also important to learn when to enact purpose and power. To be out of rhythm is to be in chaos, and not reaching one's best potential. There are certain roles that each of us must play in order to maintain harmony.

Energy is the force that has the power to change. Physicists describe energy as being either kinetic or potential. All things which were created have energy. Everything was created to make some difference. Therefore, it is necessary to use these energies wisely. Otherwise, one may come into conflict with the intent of the Creator. **Movement** is outward evidence of energy and, therefore, life.

Affect is a way of responding to and viewing one's environment as a whole. It is a recognition that "things" and people are influenced by a variety of events and forces, and typically not a single factor. An affective approach towards life tends to see life as an experience rather than a problem (Biko, 1971). This person will "feel" an experience and not just think through it. For example, a learning environment must not only have a teacher, book, etc..; it must also create a learning atmosphere. Of course, the proper environment to foster a particular outcome must be harmonious with the Cosmos, the Creator's intentions.

Communalism is a commitment to maintaining and

developing social connections and relationships. Communalism stresses that individual rights ought not intrude on social harmony. The word community itself suggests there is a "common unity" of interest and values around which a group of people have agreed. It is this social harmony which allows the trust necessary for collective work and responsibility (ujima) and accountability. The spiritual understanding of "connectedness" and the communal commitment are the basis for the African propensity to see members in the community as family, thus, development of fictive kinship (extended family) bonds. Members of a community share more than geographic proximity. They share common destiny and are accountable one to another. Therefore, it is in the best interest of everyone to see all people develop to his or her best potential (the intent of Creator). Consequently, "It takes a whole village to raise a child."

Expressive Individualism refers to the belief that each person has unique and distinctive talents which must be developed and expressed in order to bring validity and meaning to one's life. It is a notion that each person in the community has something to contribute, a unique genius, to the maintenance and development of that community.

Take, for example, jazz, where a musician or singer is encouraged to find/develop his or her own style. So whatever the musician plays or the singer sings, it becomes unique. In contrast, European classical music stresses "sameness." The goal is to play the music as closely to how it is written as possible so that there is little distinction between the composer's intentions and the musician's expression. In jazz, there is planned spontaneity, the improvisation. This not only makes each song unique, but also provides an opportunity for the participants to put their "signature" on the song. We see expressive individualism in other forms of music, particularly rap and gospel. Please carefully note that expressive individualism and communalism are not necessarily opposites. Though Theolonius Monk, Count Basie, and Joe Sample would play "A-Train" differently, they would not play the song so differently that it is no longer recognizable as "A-Train."

The individual expression must fit into the continuity of the song. Individual expression is essential to bringing new energy and genius to the community; however, that expression should not destroy the common unity. This does not mean that one can/should not challenge or question those values and interests around which common unity has been formed. Otherwise, the village becomes stagnant. The proverb, "I am because we are, we are because I am" constantly reminds us there must be balance between the community and the individual in order for both to exist.

Oral Tradition refers to the importance placed on the speaking and interpreting of words. Beyond the obvious that oral communication is an expedient way of conveying ideas, African heritage places high importance on the ability to use and interpret words creatively, to be able to choose words that communicate complex ideas in simple phrases (proverbs and parables). Thus, the importance of the griot, the story teller.

Consequently, oral tradition places high importance on the ability to understand what was said and not said, and how it was said - being able to decipher the multiple meanings of words. So that, when a person hears the proverb, "Though a log may lie in a river for 100 years, it will never become a crocodile," he or she is able to get past the obvious and apply the metaphor.

At the base of oral tradition is a belief that the spoken word carries with it positive or negative power, energy, a spirit which becomes a part of and changes the universe. Asante (1987) labels this belief as "nommo," a word from Dogon people of Mali. Nommo maintains that if parents want to rear a smart child, they ought not call the child dumb or use other terms derived from a deficiency analysis (see note 11). This is consistent with what cognitive theorists have come to realize. Language (symbols and their corresponding meaning) is necessary for logic. Therefore, the type of language to which a person is exposed will affect one's ability to form logical thought. Furthermore, if a person is to form logical thought, then it is necessary to use language that is based in his or her cultural heritage. Otherwise, one will form logic that is inconsistent with one's own existence (self-destructive). Thus, the oppressed can never use the language (symbols and their corresponding meaning) of the oppressor to obtain freedom.

Jesus addresses the power of words in Matthew 12: 33 - 37 NIV:

> 33 "Make a tree good and its fruit will be good, or make a tree bad and its fruit will be bad, for a tree is recognized by its fruit. 34 You brood of vipers, how can you who are evil say anything good? For out of the overflow of the heart the mouth speaks. 35 The good man brings good things out of the good stored up in him, and the evil man brings evil things out of the evil stored up in him. 36 But I tell you that men will have to give account on the day of judgment for every careless word they have spoken. 37 For by your words you will be acquitted, and by your words you will be condemned."

Rev. Jerome Peters (1997) in a sermon summarized:

> Jesus is alerting us to the fact of being cautious of how we speak and what we speak. Words or statements that are idly spoken expressions either to persons, about persons, or in general

conversations which are not beneficial or uplifting, such biblically unprofitable engagements must never be a practice by disciples of Jesus Christ. It is the words that we speak that will work to our condemnation or to our blessing.

My son, Tré, was born with his eyes wide open. Within three days, he could follow an object with his eyes. Shortly thereafter, a few people labeled him as "nosy." I corrected them, saying "He is inquisitive." At his age, not knowing all the proper social norms about "minding business," he was merely examining what he saw. "Nosy" has negative connotations while "inquisitive" suggests intelligence. Is it any wonder that a child who is reared in an environment where examination and inquiry are seen as negative or bothersome is likely to avoid science, math, critical thinking? The words that enter our environment will shape how we see ourselves and eventually what we will do.

Social Time Perspective is a necessary philosophical stance given the aforementioned characteristics of African centered culture and philosophy. It is a way of perceiving time as a function of environmental influences and spiritual interpretations. Social time perspective tends to see time as cyclic phenomena; time is not simply a linear march through predictable chronological units. If something is not fulfilled and "it" is meant to be, it will return, though it may return in the next generation.

Many have concluded that social time perspective is why "black folks are always late." There is some truth to that conclusion. Just because an event is scheduled to start at 2:00 p.m., there is no guarantee there will be anybody there at two, especially if the proper social cues are not present. However, for many African Americans "it's going to start late anyway" becomes a self-fulfilling and perpetuating prophecy. Having developed a self consciousness based on

America's perceptions of the inferiority of African people, many African Americans have never learned to interpret social and spiritual cues "properly." Consequently, they are often late or miss opportunities for growth.

Social time perspective is a more complex view of time than chronology. It requires a person to be able to decipher the meanings of the various phenomena surrounding a particular experience, of which chronology is one thing to consider, in order to determine if "the time is right." Thus, if a child is to be an adult at the age of eighteen, then there must be certain "things" in place socially and spiritually, which are in harmony with the Cosmos, in order for adulthood to be on time.

It is important to recognize that the whole of African centered thought and culture is not captured by these nine common themes, nor by my brief description of them. We must constantly remind ourselves that Africa is a richly diverse continent. Therefore, we need not try to oversimplify ourselves to form a homogeneous group. Africans throughout the diaspora have had experiences unique to their local and family traditions. Though we all might have used the same tools, it does not mean that we have built the same solutions. Just because I have a ball and a stick does not mean that I have to play baseball. Each family has specific experiences which have shaped the lives of its members. Consequently, there are specific lessons to be learned about how to live or not live life. And, of course, each person has had experiences where "God is trying to tell you something." For each one of us, our African experience is both collective and personal.

Family Traditions

Family traditions are those "ways" of living that

members of one's family have adapted to solve life's problems or to make life significant. Family traditions are subsets of culture, like families are subsets of the village. Where culture is the collective wisdom of the community, family traditions are the specific wisdom of people with whom one is most closely connected. Family traditions are a child's first introduction to the culture of which the family is a part - much like how one's childhood influences adulthood. Family traditions affect how one learns to relate to the village. Therefore, if family traditions are dysfunctional, not synchronized (in rhythm) with the collective cultural heritage of the village, then the children produced through such traditions are likely to be dysfunctional in their relationships with the village. Thus, the proverbs warn "The ruin of a nation starts in the homes of its people" and "The hand that rocks the cradle rules the world," suggesting that what takes place within the family will eventually affect the society and culture of which that family is a member. Given the influence of family traditions on one's development and that nothing happens without reason, it is necessary for one to study his or her family traditions in order to understand for what purpose he or she was created.

Again looking at the life of Jesus (Matthew 1 and Mark 3: 23 - 38), we see that the Old Testament is essentially the story of how God interacted with Jesus's family to set the stage for Him to come and fulfill His purpose. True Jesus is a divine being, however, the Creator is working a purpose through all our lives. The Creator has been setting into motion all necessary things to bring about fulfillment of your life's purpose. We must seek wisdom and understanding to see the Creator's plan. One way to gain insight is for a person to examine how has the Creator interacted with those people that had the most influence on that person's development. Family history and stories provide specific examples of "living life" by people with whom one has direct access.

When examining family traditions, answer the following questions: What are the recurring themes, accomplishments and struggles? How were they resolved? What was the impact on the family? These questions can help a person to understand the influences that shape his or her development, positively or negatively. Not all family traditions bring a person to the awareness of one's life's purpose. However, with sankofa (reflection, examination and action) all family traditions provide wisdom, even if it is the lesson of what not to do or what needs to be changed. By understanding the ingredients that went into a person's creation, that person can better understand for what he or she has been created. Thus, allowing him or her to better assess how prepared he or she is for fulfilling purpose.

Components of Rites of Passage

Anchored in the conceptual foundation of African cultural context and family traditions are the components of village, understanding of the rites process, and sacred knowledge. These provide a frame on which the African centered rites process can be built.

Village

The village is at the heart of the African experience, which is not surprising given the emphasis on spirituality and communalism (Biko, 1972). Africans brought to the United States did not lose the village perspective. In the book <u>Ritual: Power, Healing and Community,</u> Somé (1993) provides insight about the village community:

A true community does not need a police force. The very presence of a law enforcement system in a community is an indication that something is not working. ...A community is a place where there is consensus, not where there is a crooked–looking on looker with a gun, creating an atmosphere of unrest.... The absence of doors is not a sign of technological deprivation but an indication of the state of mind the community is in. The open mind and open heart.... Elders say that the real police in the village is spirit that sees everybody. To do wrong is to insult the spirit realm.... A functioning community is one that is its own protection. And one cannot form a community whose goal is to tear the rest of the society apart...... A true community begins in the hearts of the people involved. It is not a place of distraction but a place of being.... Finding a home is what people in community try to accomplish. In community, it is possible to restore a supportive presence for one another, rather than distrust of one another or competitiveness with one another.... The elder cannot be an elder if there is no community to make him an elder. The young boy cannot feel secure if there is no elder whose silent presence gives him hope in life. The adult cannot be who he is unless there is a strong sense of presence of the other people around. This interdependency is what I call supportive presence. (pp. 68 - 69)

For many years segregation and limited transportation technology geographically forced these elements to exist in central locations, so that people in one's neighborhood were the people with whom one was engaged in community. The people who taught the children lived next to the parents. They would attend the same church. They would have shared experiences.

However, with greater mobility the African American community is becoming more and more decentralized.

Consequently, it is less likely that a neighborhood is engaged in community. In such a situation, it is understandable why parents would not trust people in the neighborhood to participate in the rearing of their child, or other significant aspects of life.

Some (1993) states that unity of spirit, trust, openness, love and caring, respect for the elders, respect for nature, and recognition of the ancestors are the essence of the village community. These characteristics are not functions of geographic location, but of a group of people practicing them. Thus, "village" is not a geographic location, but people practicing community. Therefore, it is possible to create "village" with people who live across town or out of state. Consider churches.

Historically, African Americans have used the local church as a village, where the community worshipped the Creator; where children were dedicated, taught, tutored, and where they learned how to interact with the village. Members of a church often turned to other members for help, using the village resources; and this still continues. Though many churches are no longer "local," having members driving in from a variety of neighborhoods, still families meet in common unity, drawing upon the resources that the village provides. Churches are the places where many of our most significant rituals and ceremonies take place, providing both family tradition and community linkage for its members. In the church, African Americans have practiced respect for elders by having deaconate boards, church elders and mothers. When we take a close look at many of the churches where African Americans worship, we will tend to see the essence of the African village.

One of the primary responsibilities of the village is to provide models for living. According to social learning theorist Albert Bandura (1977, 1986), modeling is one of the basic means of learning. Bandura contends it is through visual and verbal observation that the learner forms meanings which will: 1. serve as a social prompt to initiate similar behavior in others; 2. strengthen or weaken internal models used for performance of particular behaviors; and 3. construct new symbolic representations. Bandura suggests there are three stimuli that trigger this process: 1. live models, 2. symbolic models, and 3. verbal descriptions or instructions. One example of this is when young children mimic parents' actions or repeat words they have heard. The success of the models to stimulate "making meaning" hinges upon the learner's perceived relevance and credibility of the model.

When a person wants to learn how to fly a plane, he or she will go to a flight instructor. If you want to learn math, you will go to someone who knows math. Even those who claim to be "self taught" had others whom they watched, listened to, and modeled. It is necessary for a child to see adulthood practiced in order to become a proper adult. More specifically, if an African American child is to learn to be a conscious, spiritual, productive, African American adult, that child must be in the company of conscious, spiritual, productive, African American adults. As a child even Jesus learned from his elders:

> 46 After three days they found him [Jesus] in the temple courts, sitting among the teachers, listening to them and asking them questions..... 52 And Jesus grew in wisdom and stature, and in favor with God and men (Luke 2: 46, 52 NIV).

None of us are of our own making. Consequently, it behooves the members of a community to learn and know their "role" in the village. To be engaged in "village" is to be held accountable to the members of the village for the maintenance and development of that village, by ensuring:

that the safety, energy, and potential matrix is intact; that the children receive an authentic eduction (rites of passage); and seeking wisdom from the Creator.

Village is composed of the following:

1. **Creator** is the unifying creative force in the universe. This spirit is called by a variety of names: God, Allah, Dios, Dieu, Mungu, etc.. It is the recognition of this spirit that demands harmony in the creation.

2. **Ancestors** are the members of a village or a family which have returned to the spirit world, and whose energies and accomplishments were the instruments which the Creator used to provide the f o u n d a t i o n (collective cultural wisdom) of the village. Generally, ancestors can be described as the elders of the elders. On rare occasions, a person can live so long and reach a level of spiritual awareness that he or she is considered to be a "living ancestor."

3. **Elders** are the people who have the most invested in the village and therefore are most accountable. Elders have had the time to perfect living and gain wisdom; therefore, they are typically the oldest of the living. Eldership is a position earned by sharing what one has learned and accepting accountability for the growth and development of the village.

4. **Adults (Nation Builders)** are the people who have reached a level of maturity and consciousness that makes them accountable for their actions and, thus, accountable for their contribution to the village. Adults are old enough to be accountable, yet young enough to have the energy to do what must be done.

5. **Children** are essentially adults in training. They represent the future of the village. Children are second only to the Creator as the most powerful force in the village. The health of a village can be diagnosed by the condition of the children. When elders and adults

are fulfilling their responsibilities, children are respectful to the village and Cosmos; children feel safe, and they explore and practice their unique geniuses. However, when elders and adults have not fulfilled their responsibilities, the children are disrespectful, confused, and violent (Some, 1993). Often these children have not been reconnected to the Creator. Therefore, the children will seek value and purpose in material things. In such an environment, elders and adults become afraid of their own children and bewildered. Consequently, to neglect children is to destroy the village community. All activities in a healthy village will ultimately add to the development of its children. A healthy village recognizes that the children contain within them all the village needs to exist.

6. **The Unborn** are the future generations. To recognize their existence is to have faith in the Creator to supply the village needs. Therefore, one can never "give up" on the village community, particularly the children. To "throw away" or to lose a generation, a village is likely to lose the generations to follow. Also, to recognize the unborn is to understand that one's purpose is a part of the ongoing will of the Creator. That your activities will be the foundation on which others, unknown to you, will stand (or fall). The unborn reminds us that life is not stagnant. One day we will be the ancestors. (How will we be judged?)

Process

As alluded to earlier, there are many different models on which the rites of passage process can be based; however, the process is universal. The rites of passage process consists of preparation, separation, transition and reincorporation stages (Goggins, 1996).

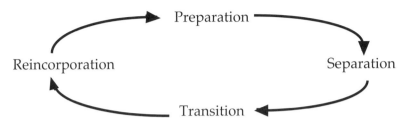

Preparation is the stage where the initiate learns what it is to be a member. The preparation stage starts with some basic assumptions about the Creator's intent. **Separation** is the stage when the initiate is tested. It is in this stage that the initiate must demonstrate the ability to fulfill his or her responsibilities within the group and within his or her particular stage of life. **Transition** is the stage in which the initiate is transformed into a member. It is the between/ betwixt. This is usually marked with a ceremony where the initiate enters as a nonmember and exits as a member. **Reincorporation** is the stage where the new member is presented back to the community. This is also the point that the new member will be accountable for his or her new responsibilities.

It is important to note that progression through these stages is not necessarily linear, nor are the stages mutually exclusive. There are many factors which will greatly influence the time spent in and emphasis on each stage. Consider marriage and high school graduation as examples.

Marriage is more than the wedding ceremony. There is a time of preparation. This is a time in which the two individuals would learn what it is to be a "good" mate. Generally, this would be within the concept of a good adult. There is a time of separation - engagement. The individuals separate themselves from other relationships. They also seek counsel from an elder (minister) who will test and approve their decision. The transition, the wedding, is the ceremony where individuals enter as not married and exit as married. Reincorporation comes at the end of the wedding ceremony. This is when the couple is introduced to the community as "Mr. and Mrs. ...." It also marks the beginning of accountability for fulfilling the responsibilities of marriage. In many cultures, marriage legitimizes parenthood; therefore, marriage is part of the preparation stage for the rites process for parenthood. So, the marriage process is not only its own rites of passage, but it is also part of another process.

Another example would be high school graduation. Preparation would be Kindergarten through 12th grade. However, preparation would also include preschool, prenatal care, all experiences which affected the education of the graduate. Separation would be exams and other tests necessary to graduate. Transition would be the graduation ceremony itself. The reincorporation stage would follow the graduation. The graduates would be expected to apply what they have learned in school to be "productive" citizens. Of course, high school is the preparation for college. The previous examples illustrate the many layers of the rites of passage process.

Rites of passage is not a simple progression through a "program," but a process which prepares a person to live life. The rites constitute a dynamic "overlapping" process, which connects past, present and future; intentions with actions; life with purpose. Therefore, it is inappropriate to refer to rites of passage as some program one would go through. Instead, rites of passage is a dynamic process which one enters. Each stage that is successfully completed provides the preparation and insight in other areas of life and eventually for future stages and challenges.

Also important to understanding the African centered rites of passage process is an understanding of rituals and ceremonies. Rituals are metaphors for philosophical principles. Consider the following examples: a) the ritual of blessing food puts into practice beliefs that one should be grateful to use God's creation - the prepared food may harbor danger and requires God's sanctification, and all "good" things come from God and therefore require acknowledgment; b) The ritual of taking attendance supports the belief that being in school is important and students should attend; c) Before I speak to a community, I will ask the elders' permission to speak. This ritual is done to show respect to the elders and supports my belief that elders should be the guardians of the community. They have (should have) the most time and effort invested in the community. They are (should be) the wise ones. Therefore, they should provide permission before anyone speaks energy (nommo) into the community. Rituals unite abstract concepts with tangible actions.

There are three types of rituals: 1) Communal; 2) Family; and 3) Individual (Some, 1993). **Communal rituals** affirm unity and cohesiveness. Every adult member of the village is obligated to perform. An example of a communal ritual would be the invocation at the beginning of a public event. The invocation is meant to draw people together under one spirit and mind, or to be "on one accord," so that they can practice village. Also, it is the time where the village/community comes before the Creator as a single entity. Other examples of communal rituals would be "fellowship time," voting, parades, block parties, and holidays. **Family rituals** provide unity and cohesiveness for family units, and are performed by family elders and every responsible family member, those initiated into adulthood. Family rituals may include such things as reunions, Sunday dinner, sitting at the adults' table or anything that the family does routinely. **Individual rituals** are those rituals which individuals must perform to maintain proper relationship with the Cosmos, such as a bedtime prayer, time spent in meditation, or a walk in the park. It is anything that a person routinely does to connect to the Cosmos and to strengthen that connection to the Cosmos.

Communal, family, and individual rituals provide consistency between the community, the family and the individual. By performing these rituals, the member demonstrates his or her ability to fulfill his or her responsibilities within that culture/society and demonstrates a commitment to the development and maintenance of the village.

Ceremonies are visual representations of what happens as a result of rituals. They mark the transition from one stage to the next. Thus, the quality of the ritual is embedded in the intent of the ceremony, and the ceremony is only justified by the successful completion of the necessary rituals. Therefore, rituals and ceremonies are only significant if they move a person though the rites process in a cultural context towards purpose (intent of the Creator). Rituals and ceremonies help us stay in "rhythm" with the Cosmos.

Sacred Knowledge

The last component necessary to frame the rites of passage experience is sacred knowledge. Sacred knowledge is the knowledge necessary in order for a person to fulfill his or her purpose at a particular stage in life. What makes the information sacred is the assumption that one's purpose is determined by the intent of the Creator, thus making one's purpose an act of God. Subsequently, any knowledge which is necessary for a person to fulfill his or her purpose is sacred. Sacred knowledge is the "special" set of meanings and wisdom; if possessed, it will transform a nonmember into a member.

Sacred knowledge is transformative. For example, sacred knowledge dynamically changes from one stage of life to another, from person to person, from time to time, and from community to community. Consider that an infant (0 - 2 years) must learn certain things to "successfully" be an infant: how to follow objects with his or her eyes; how to walk; begin to use language. As a child/person matures, the knowledge expected to be known increases. Therefore, what is considered to be necessary knowledge changes. Another example: there is a set of information I needed to possess to navigate successfully being a single man with no children. I needed another set of information to be successful as a married man with no children. And yet another set of information for a married man with a child. Though there is unique information in each set, there is also information common in each set. Each life has a rhythm, where a certain purpose must be fulfilled as a requirement during a particular stage of life. Likewise, each stage has specific sacred knowledge.

Of course, as the Creator's specific intentions change from person to person, the necessary information to fulfill those intentions changes. A medical doctor needs to know different information than a mechanical engineer. An entrepreneur needs different information than an educator. However as specific sacred knowledge can be, there is common sacred knowledge as well.

Common sacred knowledge is the knowledge necessary to exist in "proper" relationships with others in the community. Social norms such as common courtesy phrases, the proper way to address elders, family members and other members in the village, and acceptable behaviors are examples of common sacred knowledge. Also, common sacred knowledge includes information about the physical environment. For example, in an environment where there are cars, sacred knowledge includes how to cross the street. Simply, common sacred knowledge is what a member of a group is expected to know in order to contribute safely and successfully to the development and harmony of the village.

Sacred knowledge transforms the possessor of it. This transformation is evident through one's actions. Specifically, when a person's conduct is consistent with a particular "code," it suggests knowledge of and accountability to that code. Therefore, an adult must act like an adult and to act like an adult is to be knowledgeable about adulthood and to be accountable to the responsibilities of being an adult. To possess knowledge and not be transformed by it suggests that one's transformation is yet to happen. A child is being prepared to be an adult. However, some of the knowledge learned does not become necessary until the child becomes an adult.

Since sacred knowledge is so dynamic and complex, it requires elders and adults to examine constantly what are the necessary lessons of life. It is the responsibility of the elders and adults to discern the essence of sacred knowledge and determine why this knowledge is sacred. Subsequently, elders and adults must seek constantly clarification from the Creator and assess the present conditions in order to provide opportunities for the children and themselves to learn sacred knowledge. Therefore, if elders and adults are to fulfill their responsibility properly, they must be connected to the Creator. Would you go to Volkswagen to learn how to properly maintain a car built by General Motors? In other words, if we (elders and adults) are to rear children properly to fulfill the mission the Creator has created the children for, then we consult the Creator of the children in order to discern what the children must know. It is the wisdom of the Creator as it has been demonstrated through the ancestors, through the Cosmos, and through meditation/reflection/inquiry which allows elders and adults to see the essence of sacred knowledge.

To determine and evaluate the essence of sacred knowledge, a person must be able to discern the lesson to be learned. For example, there was a time when the Maasai would require their group of warrior initiates to kill a lion. By our standards (African Americans in 1997), on the surface this may seem brutal. However, closer examination reveals something more profound. The Maasai place a high value on cattle and live on the savanna (grass lands); therefore, it is very likely that a Maasai will have to protect his cattle from a lion. Thus, being prepared to do so is wise. However, there are still even deeper lessons in this ritual such as: working in groups; learning the methods of the enemy; and bravery in the face of fierce opposition. It is these lessons which are at the foundation of the essence of that sacred knowledge of how to kill a lion. The elders and adults of a village are responsible for determining which lessons are still necessary. Furthermore, how are those lessons to be taught and what rituals and ceremonies will be used to teach those lessons? The elders and adults may decide to continue the ritual or create a new one.

Many African American adults and elders decided that their children would not have to "go through what I went through," forgetting that what they went through taught them valuable lessons about how to live life. It is perfectly normal to want to protect one's child from the cruelty of a racist and oppressive society. However, the African proverb warns, "When you take a knife away from a child, give him a piece of wood instead." It is not good enough to take away something bad, but it must be replaced by something constructive. In the case of the generations that came into adulthood during the times of social struggle and then decided to shield their children from society's opposition, they did a disservice to their children if they did not provide other opportunities for the children to learn what can be learned when people struggle together. As Frederick Douglass suggested, "Where there is no struggle there is no progress." Of course, parents do not want a child to struggle with hunger, poverty, poorly equipped schools, drugs, racism and discrimination. However, those who experienced these "lions," and were able to survive, learned things like: how to make a meal out of bare cupboards; working together for a cause greater than oneself; that preparation, effort and opportunity are connected; and faith in the Creator to create a way out of no way.

Though elders and adults may wish to abandon certain rituals or conditions, they must be careful to examine the essence of such experiences, determine if the knowledge learned from such experiences is still needed, and, if so, then create new rituals which teach the necessary knowledge in order for the children to be prepared to fulfill the intent of their Creator. For example, if the elders and adults of a village decide that confronting a lion is no longer necessary, but still agree that the lessons of bravery, camaraderie, and strategic planning are important to adulthood, they might replace confronting lion rituals with organizing and implementing a needed community service or event. Or elders and adults may decide that learning computers is as important to survival in the 21st century as learning how to hunt in previous years. It is also important to note that sacred knowledge will change over time. What was needed to be known 20 years ago may not be necessary today. At an Urban League dinner, Dr. Robert L. Hewitt summarized this concept in the statement, "We have to adjust to changing times, while maintaining unchanging principles." To recognize sacred knowledge is to recognize the need for specific means of transmitting specific knowledge. Transmission can be secret or open; written or oral; formal or informal, but it must be. It is only through the rites of passage process and its supporting spiritual/philosophical structures that a person can know and ultimately fulfill the Creator's intentions for his or her life.

Transformative Power of Rites of Passage

NKYIN KYIN (Changing One's Self)

HWEHWEMUDUA
(Searching Rod or Measuring Rod)
Excellence, Perfection, Knowledge and
Superior Quality

The very purpose of the rites of passage process is to transform the initiate into a person who can meet the demands of his or her life's calling (i.e., the intent of the Creator). Hence, the significance of a rites of passage process can be measured by its power to cause or facilitate change in one's skills and/or insight.

The Bible is filled with persons undergoing transformation from one stage of life to another: Abraham, Moses, David, Paul and, of course, Jesus provide some of the most poignant examples. In Genesis 17, Abram and Sarai are given new names of Abraham and Sarah to mark the transition when God (Creator) revealed the "new" intent for their lives. From his birth and to his death, the books of Exodus, Numbers and Deuteronomy chronicle the transformations in Moses's life. One can clearly see that at each stage Moses is being prepared for future challenges. Likewise, 1 Samuel 16 to 1 Kings 2 records significant moments in the transformation of David from a child to a king.

The conversion of Saul to Paul dramatically illustrates the power of the rites of passage process. As Saul, he zealously persecuted Christians. Learning the critical issues about Christianity such as philosophy, where it was spreading and where it was not, its organizational structures, what was its "most" convincing points, and what to say to discourage people from converting to Christianity were important to Saul's success. However, this stage of his life proved to be preparation for "being" Paul. The road to Damascus was the separation stage. The transition stage was while he was blind, and reincorporation stage began when the scales fell from his eyes. Having completed the "rites" process, Paul was transformed into the prolific biblical author and arguably the person most responsible for "organizing" the early Christian church by drawing upon the knowledge and skills developed as Saul. Illustrations of the transformative power of rites of passage are not limited to Biblical characters.

In <u>Narrative of Frederick Douglass: An American Slave</u>, Douglass reflects on the "significant" moments of his life such as being separated from his mother as a child, watching brutal beatings, learning how to read and write, leading an insurrection, and escaping from slavery and how these experiences influenced his philosophy and actions against slavery. In <u>The Confessions of Nat Turner</u> (Khalifah, 1993), Turner recalls the significant moments which led to his insurrection - a two-day war on South Hampton County. Turner states: "In my childhood a circumstance occurred which made an indelible impression on my mind, and laid the groundwork of that enthusiasm [the insurrection]..." (p. 16). Turner remembered that his father and mother had told him that he was intended for some great purpose. Also, he remembered his grandmother saying, "Nat had too much sense to be raised [in slavery], and if he was, he would never be of any service to anyone as a slave" (p.16). Again and again, autobiographies and books like <u>Growing Up Black</u>, edited by Jay David, and <u>Children of the Dream: The Psychology of Black Success</u> by Audrey Edwards and Dr. Craig K. Polite, document "successful" African Americans' reflections on significant moments that transformed their thinking and personal development.

In an interview on BET Talk, July 8, 1997, Geronimo (Pratt) Ji Jaga was asked, "How did you keep the faith [during his wrongful incarceration]?" He replied, "I was prepared by the elders." Likewise, when a member of the "Little Rock Nine" was asked about how they were able to withstand the hatred while integrating Central High School, she replied "We had no choice! We were chosen by our community and were prepared to face the crowds."

As alluded to earlier, when a person recognizes that the present is connected to the past and future, and recognizes that the past and present experiences are preparation for future experiences, then "full" transformative power of rites of passage can take effect. So when a person finds himself or herself in circumstances for which he or she has not been prepared, he or she has the consciousness to examine, "What happened?", "Why?", or "What am I doing here?"

Consider the parable of the "lost son" (Luke 15: 11-32). It is his recognition that he had not been prepared to live his life in a pig sty which is the impetus for deciding to return home. Here again it is important to note that rites of passage does not prevent a person from straying from his or her intended purpose. However, the rites of passage process does ensure that if a person strays from his or her intended purpose, then that person knows that he or she has strayed.

A child reared in a family where: a) the child is expected to fulfill the Creator's intent for that child's life; b) the elders and adults of the child's family maintained a relationship with the Creator so that they can discern the Creator's intent for the child; and c) the child's family elders and adults provided the opportunities to know the Creator, discern the Creator's specific intent for his or her life, and develop necessary skills and knowledge, will have a standard by which he or she can evaluate circumstances, experiences and concepts.

American education philosopher John Dewey (1938/ 1963) suggested that purpose is the criterion necessary to determine intelligence (the means by which one strategizes to execute purpose) and discipline (the ability to follow one's strategy). Hence, to be without purpose is to be without intelligence and discipline. Conversely, to enter an African centered, family based, community linked rites of passage, which connects a person to his or her life's purpose, is to develop intelligence and discipline.

Highlights of my rites of passage (thus far)

To discuss the highlights of my rites of passage process, it is necessary for me to start in the fall of 1992, when I was formally trained in African centered rites of passage facilitation and instruction. I was introduced to Dr. Anthony Mensah's model which is based on the Akan traditions of Ghana. The information I received during the training allowed me to reflect on my life. I then realized that my family had provided many of the same experiences and information, thus, a rites of passage. Though my family did not call the experiences they provided rites of passage, nor had they been formally introduced to the concepts of rites of passage, they still managed to provide the basic concepts and experiences of an African centered, family based, community linked rites of passage.

The Osborne family traditions were transmitted through rituals, stories and land. One of the rituals practiced by my mother was routinely calling home (Grambling, LA) at 7:30 a.m. every Saturday. Another was traveling home for holidays (it was what made the holidays special). These rituals stressed the importance of being connected to family. Also, they were metaphors for the importance of seeking counsel from and accountability to family elders, and the importance of returning home.

While at my grandparents' house, one ritual in which everyone is expected to participate is a small devotion conducted around the dining table. Every morning before breakfast, everyone met around the table and held hands; then either "grandpa" or "grandma" would read from the Bible; then grandma would request for someone to say the family prayer; then all others would say a Bible verse; and devotion ended with everyone saying "Amen" and hugging each other. This ritual is meant to focus everyone's attention on the importance of family connection as well as the individual's connection to the Creator, specifically though Christian teachings and philosophies.

Another significant tradition in the family is land. Whenever my mother and I went home, we would find the time to go "down home" to Saint Rest. This is a small community where my matriarchal ancestors have owned land since 1865. It is the site of the Osbornes' (grandfather) and the Leonards' (grandmother) family graveyards, churches and reunions. Saint Rest is where my mother was born, where my grandfather grew up and met my grandmother, where my great great grandfathers farmed land and are buried. Being surrounded by family history provided the impetus for storytelling. The stories had themes such as faith in God, farming (land ownership), independence, masonry, education, community service, excellence, and family interdependence. To be a descendant of Moses Osborne is to have at least an appreciation of such concepts. This was most clear during a ceremony for my cousin Kay and myself. We were the first in our generation to graduate from college. To mark the transition, a ceremony was organized where Kay and I sat in the middle of a circle of family and friends. Each adult told a story about when we were children, then gave some advice or charge for the future. Once every adult had spoken, our grandfather laid hands on us, prayed for us, pronounced us to be adults, and charged us to be successful and live a good life.

My father's family told stories and traditions that focused on faith, ingenuity, hard work and education, as well. My father, who has earned three terminal degrees - Ph.D., Ed.D. and Ed.S. - told stories about working "odd jobs" and playing in a jazz band to pay for college. This is consistent with one of my grandfather's favorite sayings: "It may take faith the size of a mustard seed to move a mountain, but you had better bring a shovel." Altogether, the stories of my ancestors' and elders' lives and the rituals which symbolized their beliefs helped me to understand my life. Being connected to one's ancestors and being connected to cultural heritage are important concepts in African centered, family based, community linked rites of passage; however, not just to the African experience in the United States. One must be connected to the African experience in Africa. One way my parents provided this for me was a trip to Africa. My father, mother and I spent 4 weeks touring the continent. I had my 9th birthday there. We visited many countries: Senegal, where I went to Goree Island, stood in the dungeon and looked out the door of "no return"; Ivory Coast; Benin; Liberia; Nigeria; Tanzania, where I saw the oldest human remains which had been found (in 1975) at Olduvai Gorge; Kenya, where I went to Ngornongaro Crater wildlife reserve; and Ethiopia, where I saw one of the oldest continuous Christian churches in the world, from which a monk was sent to convert barbarians (see note 12) to Christianity. During our time in Africa, we visited villages, cities, rural areas and universities. These experiences had a profound influence on my life.

For the first time I could see the contradictions of how people in the United States perceived Africa, and its reality. (Remember I am nine years old.) In the United States, Africa is one big jungle, but I stood in modern cities. In the United States, the lion was "king of the jungle"; in Africa, lions live on savannas. If the oldest human remains are in Kenya and Tanzania, then why every time I saw Adam and Eve were they white? If one of the oldest Christian churches in the world is in Ethiopia and from this region monks were sent to convert the barbarians in northern Europe to Christianity, how can Christianity be the "White man's" religion? Not only did these experiences challenge what I believed about Africa and African people (and by extension myself), but these experiences provided a basis for reinterpreting the world and my place in it. After returning,

I began to question my teachers and the motives for their presentations, particularly when it pertained to Africa and African people. I would let them know I had pictures to prove what they were saying was not always true. Some of my teachers thought I had been "ruined." I questioned not only information about Africa and African people, but how could Columbus discover America if there were people already here, and how could Lewis and Clark discover the West if they had a guide? Furthermore, I began to question the counselors and others in the schooling system: "Why would African people be misrepresented?" As I wrote in African Centered Rites of Passage and Education,

> I came to the conclusions: 1) that people misrepresent the "truth" because they are ignorant or do not want to face effects/affects of the "truth"; and 2) the information presented in schools and media was a reflection of interpretations not absolutes.

It is important for balance to point out that some of the things I learned from my family was "what not to do," and even with a "culturally rich" background, I managed to flunk out of college my freshman year. However, it was because of this background I knew that I could and had to graduate from college, and I did (Jan. 1990). I have gone on to complete a Master's degree, and I am currently finishing a Doctorate.

It was not until I had become conscious of the rites of passage process, in November 1992, that I could more fully appreciate the role my family traditions and African cultural heritage played in my ability to critically think and reinterpret information. And, with this new "light," I could better discern the Creator's intent for my life. Subsequently, I have gained greater focus and "power."

Another significant transition that has brought new

levels of insight has been fatherhood. The birth of my son has brought a level of love, commitment and purpose I could have never imagined possible. Watching him, I see gifts and energies that must be honed and disciplined. It becomes obvious to me that he is not simply a creation of Dietra and myself, but he came here equipped for a purpose. At two years old, he is already manifesting many "raw" talents and energies.

It is this understanding of his creation that demands of me accountability to his Creator. My son is not mine to make of him what I will. Though I have authority over him, I am in partnership with the Creator to effect his future, and will be cursed if I do not hold up my end of the bargain. To provide him with the necessary experiences to develop his intent is a daunting task. However, as I am coming into greater understanding of my son's life purpose, it elevates and motivates me to become better in tune to the Creator and a better person. One way that I come to know the Creator's intention for my son's life is to examine carefully his personality and how I "know" him (Appendix 2).

Knowledge of one's purpose is critical to developing character and discipline. It is through the pursuit of one's purpose that personality is tested and refined. In <u>Pursuit of Purpose</u>, Myles Munroe (1992) discusses the characteristics of purpose. He states, "Everything has a purpose, which determines its status in relationship to everything else." Munroe argues:

> Life with purpose is precise and directed. Life without purpose is depressing.... Purpose protects you from being busy but not effective... Purpose serves as a guide for determining the best path to a predetermined end... Life without specific measurable objectives is [at best] vague and haphazard... Purpose propels those who are committed to God's [Creator's] plans

through the worst of experiences. (pp. 81 - 92)

Munroe's arguments are consistent with the works of Frankl (1962) and contemporary researchers who have found that people who have a sense of purpose tend to be happier; live longer with a better quality of life; are less likely to suffer from depression and other neurological diseases such as Alzheimer's; and less likely to engage in self-destructive behaviors (i.e., suicide, smoking, drug and alcohol abuse). Therefore, one of the most significant aspects of the transformative power of African centered, family based, community linked rites of passage is rooted in the ability of the "rites" process to connect an individual to his or her purpose. It is this connection which helps to bring sanity and serenity to a person as he or she confronts the obstacles and disappointments that "life" sometimes brings; sanity and serenity even in the midst of a sexist and racist society that is determined to dehumanize people of African descent.

Another aspect of transformative power is the social bonds that are created and nurtured by the rites of passage process. Jomo Kenyatta (1962), describing the Gikuyu community system of education (family-based community-linked rites of passage), states:

The first and most obvious principle of educational value which we see in the Gikuyu system of education is that the instruction is always applied to an individual's concrete situation; behavior is taught in relation to some particular person.... the African is taught how to behave to father or mother, grandparents, and to other members of the kinship group.... The striking thing in the Gikuyu system of education and the feature which most sharply distinguishes it from the European system of education is the primary place given to personal relations.... While the Westerner asserts that character formation is the chief thing, he forgets that character is formed primarily through relations with other people, and that there is no other way in which it can grow. (pp. 116 - 117)

It is these social bonds that support the practicing of village and add to the resiliency of the person participating in the family-based community-linked rites of passage process.

The combinations of sense of purpose and supportive educational social bonds are important factors in the development of responsible, ethical and problem-solving adults. These factors encourage the family and community to accept responsibility and accountability for each child's learning and healthy development. This in turn fosters families and community to set high expectations, monitor the learning process, and intervene when problems arise for every child.

Families and, thus, communities that are actively providing family-based, community-linked rituals and ceremonies are likely to reduce the need for unsanctioned, dangerous, and self-destructive rituals, such as gang initiation and drug (alcohol) abuse. Sense of purpose, foundations for critical thinking, supportive social bonds, and high expectations for success are the compelling forces in the transformative power of African centered, family based, community linked rites of passage.

Thus far, I have discussed the transformative power of African centered, family based, community linked rites of passage as it primarily pertains to an individual or family. However, there is at least one other very important consideration: the growth towards "critical mass" as more families and individuals become aware of the African centered rites of passage process, and begin to practice

African centered, family based, community linked rituals and develop ceremonies to mark the transitions into new stages of consciousness and responsibility.

Critical mass is a principle that requires a certain amount of "something" to be present before a self-sustaining chain reaction will occur. Translated into social theory, critical mass is the certain number of people who are practicing a unique behavior needed to change the behavior of the total population so that the new behavior is self-perpetuating. Take, for example, the "high five." The first time I saw it was on TV in a football game. After someone scored, a group of players (brothers) did the little dance, jumped up and did the high five. As more and more people copied these players, a critical mass of the population was reached, and eventually the people giving "high fives" were not copying the original football players. It was something that was just done. And today, most people probably cannot imagine a time where there was no "high five." Likewise, as more people become familiar with the African centered rites of passage process, there will come a time in which it will spread. Those who do not practice it will be thought of as odd, and the general population will assume that African centered rites of passage has always been practiced by the masses.

Therefore, as people concerned about the African centered rites of passage movement, and as people who understand the essential need for this process to be a part of the African American experience, by simply practicing it, you are participating in the transformation of the African American community.

Constructing African Centered Family Based Community Linked Rites of Passage

Thus far, I have discussed the concepts and components that form the family-based and community-linked African-centered rites of passage process. In this chapter, I will discuss some strategies and steps for implementing these concepts and components to create a rites of passage process. Again, I would like to reiterate that the purpose of this book is to provide you with the necessary information in order for you to create an African centered rites of passage process that is based upon the family traditions of the initiate(s) and link the initiate(s) to their respective communities and ultimately to the African diaspora. It is not my intention to provide a "ready made kit." It is your responsibility to construct the specific rituals and ceremonies. Also understand that all the concepts, components, and the following strategies and activities are a part of the rites of passage process. There is no set order to which they must be completed. This is a dynamic and often fluid process. As one sister once said, "We must plan our work and work our plan at the same time." So to this end, I suggest the following strategies and considerations.

Identify the elders and adults of the initiate(s) who are willing to be accountable for providing the proper education (rites of passage) for the initiate(s). Idealistically, included in this group are the parents and grandparents of the initiate(s). It is this "collective" that will directly serve as guides through the various stages of the rites of passage process for the initiate(s). It is important to recall the proverb "You can not teach what you do not know; you can not lead where you will not go." Thus, to serve as guides, one must be familiar with the African centered rites of passage process and model the process as well.

The guides must create opportunities to recognize, reflect and discuss amongst themselves how the rites of passage process has impacted their lives, both as individuals and collectively. If none of the guides has been formally trained in rites of passage facilitation and instruction, it would be wise to seek the aid of a "certified" instructor or at least someone with firsthand experience. The ongoing discussion between the guides should examine and nurture their partnership with the Creator, so that each guide can "better" discern individually and collectively their responsibilities. Also, the guides should discuss the eleven basic assumptions of the African centered rites of passage process (pages 10 - 13). The guides should restate the assumptions in their own words and discuss other basic assumptions they believe should be a part of the process. Other considerations are the contributions of the ancestors and the impact of the group's/family's decisions on the children's children.

To examine the contributions of the ancestors is not only to learn historical facts, but includes understanding how the ancestors' activities (scholarship, sciences, arts, sports, philosophy, industry, math, etc..) shape "our" daily lives. In other words, take time to learn that Garret Morgan invented the gas mask and the traffic light and that the concepts of algebra, trigonometry and geometry were developed in ancient KMT (Kemet or Egypt). And, take the time to explore the question, "What influences did these inventions and concepts have on our community and world?" Another aspect of examining the contributions of the ancestors is to identify how Africans throughout the diaspora express African philosophy. How do we express our spirituality? In what ways do we show expressive individualism? These are the types of questions the guides must explore. What will often happen is a recognition that African Americans are more African than many of "us" realize or care to admit. It is important to understand that neither slavery nor the middle passage destroyed "us." Neither were we created by nor did we come from slavery. Some would have us to believe that "We [African Americans] here are the children of the New World, children of a different kind", (Ralph Wiley, 1994; What Black People Should Do Now.) We are Africans with a "new world" experience. Slavery was an experience we went *through*. Our ancestors did not lose their humanity or their culture; the way we tend to do things is proof of that.

Connecting to the ancestors and understanding their contributions are not just done by the collective to "well" known ancestors, but by the individuals to their respective family ancestors. Individuals should be aware that connecting to one's ancestors may not always be easy or pleasant. However, if one remembers to focus on what can be learned, then "uncovering" troubling issues is often bearable. Of course, some issues may require professional help.

Understanding the contributions and influences of the ancestors helps us to see what is possible. By understanding the "ingredients" that went into creating the moment, the collective can better understand for what "a time like this" has been created, and therefore what must be done.

The collective must also regularly discuss its role in creating the future in which the children's children (i.e., the unborn) must live. It is imperative that the guides consider how their actions will contribute to or subtract from future generations. Being "mindful" of their impact on future generations will help the guides govern their actions and discern what the parents of future generations (i.e., the children) must learn. Thus, what must be taught.

Another important topic for discussion is the definitions and expectations for the various members of the village/family. What is the role of the Creator and of the ancestors? Who are the elders? What are their responsibilities in this village/family? How do we know them to be elders? Similar questions ought to be discussed for other members of the village (i.e., adults and children). Discussing the contributions of the ancestors, the impact on the unborn, and the various responsibilities of the members in the village/family will help the collective to monitor the matrix and identify friends, allies and enemies. As mentioned before, one of the functions of village is to provide concrete examples (models) of what is possible and the philosophic principles on which the village is based. The adults and elders become metaphors for the principles of truth, justice, righteousness, order, harmony and reciprocity (Ma'at); African cultural heritage; and ultimately for the Creator. Therefore, modeling is not to be taken lightly. There is no room for "Do as I say and not as I do." Subsequently, there must be a code of conduct which adults and elders agree to follow.

The code of conduct should be based upon the beliefs about moral behavior, responsibilities of the members of a group or family, and how they should relate to one another. The code of conduct can not be so rigid that it does not allow for expressive individualism and must be applied humbly, with the understanding that only the Creator is wise enough to pass judgment. The ancestors have provided excellent starting points for discerning proper conduct, one of which is the 42 admonitions or negative confessions of Ma'at (appendix 3), written approximately 1,500 years before the Ten Commandments by ancient Kemites (Egyptians).

The code of conduct provides a gauge by which a member can determine how well he or she is fulfilling his or her role in the village and ultimately in the Cosmos. Code of conduct may not be a formal document, but it should provide a clear understanding of acceptable behavior, responsibility, and accountability. In light of the rites of passage process, in order to be held accountable to the code of conduct, one must be prepared to do so. The rite of passage process also implies that "preparedness" takes place in stages, so there are distinctions between persons of different stages of life and consciousness. Acceptable behavior and responsibilities change from child to adult and from adult to elder *(Please note I did not include accountability. It does not change. Regardless of one's age, he or she can be held accountable for those things for which one is responsible).* In fact, it is one's preparation and ability to demonstrate knowledge of the code of conduct that distinguishes his or her stage of life, regardless of age. Age only provides a clue to where a person should be, but it does not determine one's stage of life. Subsequently, it is the code of conduct that becomes the foundation for education, the preparation and separation stages of the rites of passage process (Goggins, 1996).

The discussions I have suggested must be done honestly, openly and over a period of time. These discussions will provide the "authentic experiences" through which village can be formed. I used authentic experiences to suggest that merely calling a meeting on or just talking about rites does not prepare one to practice village. These experiences must connect members at spiritual levels. The time necessary for these discussions greatly depends upon the amount of shared experiences and philosophies between the group of people wishing to form a collective. In a family where many of the components and concepts of rites of passage are already in practice, it may only be a matter of becoming conscious of the process and deciding to recognize it formally. Conversely, a community organization may take as long as a year or more of monthly meetings. Also, time will often "wash out" those who are not serious about or can not devote the necessary time to the rites of passage process. Once having ample time to discuss and experience important issues, the collective of guides forms the core around which the village can be built.

By putting into practice those concepts on which the collective has reached consensus, they have essentially

created rituals. Some rituals are best formalized by a ceremony, while some rituals are best practiced "informally." The vast majority of rituals which comprise the rites of passage process are done informally. This does not lessen their importance in any way. Informal rituals emphasize the "day to day" state of things. This may include common courtesy, i.e., please, thank you, etc...; referring to elders as Baba, Mzee, Nana, Sir, Ma'am, Mr., and Mrs.; referring to peers as Brother, Sister; taking the time to reflect at the end of the day by prayer, meditation or writing in a journal. Informal rituals are generally performed between individuals or alone. Informal rituals help to maintain basic relationships between individuals and between an individual and his or her self. Informal rituals make the philosophic principles they represent routine and commonplace.

Formal rituals are directly associated with a particular ceremony, which marks a special occasion or a once in a lifetime event. For example, the transition from a child to an adult, or when a student graduates from high school (or college). Also, formal rituals are performed to invoke sacred place and time, or in remembrance of an important event or person, such as invocation prayer and/or libations. Formal rituals are generally performed in public settings, and are meant to connect individuals to a common mindset.

Another consideration is the age of the initiates and their state of consciousness. There are certain rituals which cannot be realistically performed if the initiate has not developed the necessary motor skills and/or mental tools. The guides must ensure that their expectations can be realistically obtained. If the initiates do not have the mental and physical tools or have not been prepared to accomplish what is expected successfully, the initiate(s) will become frustrated.

As the saying goes, "You can't run before you walk." This is not to suggest that "running" should not be a long term goal, just that the expectation to run must include preparation to walk. Also, that those who would help this person to run should know how to evaluate if the person is ready to practice running or perfect his or her walking. The issue is the guides ensuring developmentally appropriate instruction for each of the initiates. Therefore, the guides must get to know the initiates. What I am suggesting is much more than formal introductions. As aforementioned, the guides must examine all aspects of knowing the initiates. I wrote an essay on how I got to know my son (appendix 2). The guides may not write something as formal as an essay. However, they must carefully examine their interpretations of what the Creator has intended for the particular initiate, and a part of that is knowing the initiate. The "know" I suggest is a careful ongoing discussion, an exploration and evaluation with the initiate about his or her talents, strengths and weaknesses.

Even an infant will provide insights to the Creator's intentions for his or her life. For example, when we took my son to the pediatrician, one of the things she and the nurses would comment on was how he would try to lift his head until he was exhausted. They took this as a sign of his determination. This raw energy to fight against the odds or to make what he wanted to happen can be potentially a good thing; if this energy is disciplined and honed it can develop into persistence and self determination. If not disciplined, then this energy can lead to stubbornness, being "hard headed," or having an unwillingness to compromise and cooperate. Raw talents and energies refer to characteristics which need to be honed and disciplined in order to bring about positive results. Likewise, if these raw energies are not disciplined and developed, they can be destructive. Since we know that "The Creator does not create for failure" and that "Every person has the capacity to succeed," then these raw talents and energies provide insight to his potential, therefore demanding of his guides to provide experiences where these raw energies can be honed and disciplined. It is the responsibility of the guides to recognize these traits, which can be done through observation and understanding human development.

As earlier mentioned, one of the most significant findings in human development is the recognition of "windows of opportunity" in the brain. Research reveals that during the first ten years of life the brain continues to actively develop. For example, the brain grows three times its original size in the first year after birth. During this time period rituals should primarily consist of ensuring proper diet. Not only does the brain develop in terms of its size, density and weight, but also in its functions.

The brain is a dynamic and adaptive organ which will literally change in its chemical and physical structure in response to the experiences it encounters in order to deal more efficiently with similar future experiences. The brain does not automatically know how to walk, talk, have eye-hand coordination, deal with emotions; it must learn. By learning the simple and then the complex, the brain develops networks between its various parts and cells. The networks that are most used are the networks that will remain, while those networks that are not used will fade away.

The windows of opportunities represent time periods when the brain is more receptive to forming certain connections. However, with some functions, the windows of opportunity are the only times in which connections can be made (Nash, 1997). It is as if the brain is introducing itself and developing a relationship with the body in which it finds itself.

From birth to 8 years, the brain is wiring vision, developing its visual acuity. Specifically from age 1 to 3, a child is perfecting his or her binocular vision (the ability to focus both eyes on a single object near and far). From birth through 10 years, the brain is wiring feeling. The neuro-connections for stress response and eventually for more complex emotions are developing. Having a child examine his or her own feelings and responses are important. It is also more important than ever to ensure the child feels safe.

From before birth to 9 years, the brain is wiring for speech recognition. During this time period, the brain is developing the connections needed to decipher and reproduce speech. Particularly for infants, the high pitched "singsong" speech helps babies connect words with objects. However, it is important to use words and not "babble." Also, it is in this window of opportunity where other languages are best taught. The further one is removed from this window, the harder it is to learn other languages. Likewise, it is in this window where a child learns syntax (how to use words properly).

From birth to beyond 10 years, the brain is wiring for movement skills. This process develops in a three stage process. From birth to 8 years, a child is developing gross motor (big movement) skills; from 2 to 10 years, a child is developing fine motor skills; from 6 on, a child is developing "music fingering" or very fine coordinated motor skills. In this window, it is important for a child to move, dance, walk, run, pick up things, and manipulate objects with his or her hands.

The implication for guides working with young children is that certain activities should coincide with the respective window of opportunity in order to best take advantage of the brain's readiness to learn certain information and functions. For example, activities which require an initiate to focus on and follow an object (a rolling ball) and eventually eye-hand coordination (game of catch) are best taught between the ages of birth to 8 years. The neuro-connections of this stage and the movement window lay the foundations for more complex thought and functions, such as those necessary for playing music. **Another important transition in the body is adolescence.** Only the first two years of life brings more dramatic changes in physical and personality development than the changes during adolescence. There are growth spurts, increase in hormones, and new body functions to adjust to and learn. I believe it is the Creator speaking to us through our body. It is no accident that once the brain has developed basic neuro-connections needed for life, then the physical transition into adulthood begins. Therefore, guides working with young children must see adolescence as an upcoming marker. And those who are working with initiates in adolescent stage must help them through the new emotions and body functions. This is also the time in which there is the transfer of accountability and responsibility. Therefore, lessons on such subjects as time management, dating, and hygiene are appropriate.

However, not only should the guides be mindful of the internal processes of the initiate; it is also important that rituals and ceremonies coincide with the external activities in which the initiates participate. For example, it would be wise to plan to have rituals to culminate with a ceremony in the same year when a student graduates from preschool to kindergarten to the first grade or high school to college. This way school is seen as a significant part of the development into adulthood.

It should be well understood that the American schooling system was not meant to educate African Americans to be conscious of the intent of the Creator or prepared to fulfill it (Goggins, 1996). By incorporating the schooling experience into the African centered, family based, community linked rites of passage process, guides can more proactively monitor the experiences and information presented by the school system, even if it is understanding why "mistruths" are taught. In this way the initiates and guides can develop strategies to succeed in the midst of such a system.

Incorporating the schooling experience into the African centered, family based, community linked rites of passage process helps to ensure that the initiates' education is synchronous with his or her purpose. School should be thought of only as a part of the process, only one of many sources of educative experiences. The guides are responsible for setting the educational agenda (curriculum, individual education plan) of the initiate(s). To provide an African centered rites of passage process is to understand that education starts long before a child enters a school system and continues long after a student leaves a school building.

The educational agenda or individual educational plan I refer to is a strategic plan to prepare the initiate to fulfill the Creator's intent for his or her life. This plan is based on the guides' observations (discussions with) of the initiates, assumptions of appropriate behavior and insight gained through the guides' relationship with the Creator. Again, I reiterate that preparing an initiate to fulfill the Creator's intent for his or her life is a sacred activity, and the knowledge necessary to fulfill the Creator's intent is sacred as well. Hence, "we" ought not ever leave the sacred to the profane.

For older initiates, the educational plan may consist of exercises and lessons which allow the initiate to break down misconceptions, reflect and reconnect to the Cosmos in "truth." However, for youth, the educational plan will be more encompassing. For example, in light of the rites of passage process. I know that my son's high school graduation is connected to his activities at two years old. So, if I expect for him successfully to complete calculus by the 12th grade, then I must prepare him now by taking into account his talents and energies; providing opportunities to construct and practice math and inquiry skills; and "effectively" confront anything or anyone who would hinder his progress. I can not wait until he is in high school to be concerned about his classes. Nor should I leave his preparation to chance. As his primary guides (i.e., his mother, his grandparents and myself), we must ensure that the school system helps us to provide the education Tre' (my son) needs, while not allowing the school system to set the standard for Tre's education - we should expect **more**. It should be understood by the guides that to take such a stand is to take responsibility and accountability for the educative process.

Though much of my discussion has focused on the development of youth, there are significant transitions in adulthood for which an African centered, family based, community linked rites of passage is still appropriate as well. The obvious transitions are marriage and parenthood, but some other significant transitions include: career development, economic planning/investing/development, home ownership, and eldership. All of these require some preparation and have impact on the family, community and future generations.

As alluded to earlier, there have been many scholars who have suggested there are several stages which constitute the life cycle. Each stage can be characterized by its particular challenge.

Age Group	Basic Challenge	Primary Task
Birth - 11	Growth	Develop curiosity/ critical inquiry skills; Develop imagination and interest; Develop communication and social skills; Develop talents

12 - 14	Transition	
15 - 25	Exploration	Clarifying values; Developing Life Strategies; Implementation
26 - 30	Transition	
31 - 40	Establishment	Stabilizing Resources; Focusing Efforts Advancement
41 - 45	Transition	
46 - 60	Maintenance	Perfecting, Updating Skills and Innovation
61 - 65	Transition	
66 +	Eldership	Leadership, Guidance

The previous table is meant to provide benchmarks. The suggested age groups are estimates and not "set in stone." Nor are the challenges and tasks mutually exclusive to these age groups. Remember, rites of passage is a process which connects the beginning to the end and eventually to the beginning again. This historical continuity is an understanding that past, present and future are connected - that one can not take place without the other. Life is a continuous interrelated and interdependent phenomena. Life is not a series of isolated events, but a series of proleptic moments, so that movement through these stages is a matter of degrees, or becoming. For example, a person who is a parent at 25 has more "eldership" responsibilities than a 25 year old who is not a parent. However, all people in the village/family, except among the youngest, have some kind of eldership responsibilities to those younger or less experienced. In the African centered, family based, community linked rites of passage process, we are all in a state of becoming an elder, though it may not be our primary challenge.

Another question may be how often should rituals and ceremonies be conducted? Remember that the rites of passage process is a way of life, which is meant to bring an initiate into knowledge of and prepare him or her for his or her given purpose. Therefore, the rites of passage process should be practiced everyday. With young children, many of the rituals are teaching common courtesy and basic skills. So idealistically, setting a special time each day for lessons would be appropriate. Obviously with collectives which are community based, it may only be possible to meet once a week or biweekly. Whatever the case, the lessons should be consistent. However, as children mature and their cognitive skills develop, special lessons can be spaced out to the point where initiates may need to come together only once a month. Of course the time which is set aside depends on the collective and the initiate(s). In some cases, there will be a need to teach at moments that are outside of the planned lesson. These "teachable moments" should not be missed.

Where to Start?!

The first set of rituals a child ought to be exposed, to is prenatal care. This should include medical care, nutrition, playing music with complex rhythms and melodies and smooth transitions for the baby, such music as jazz (Joe Sample, Stanley Jordan), and talking and reading to the baby. Obviously, if you are working with initiates who have already made the transition from the unborn to the born, prenatal care would not be appropriate, though developing a schedule for routine medical care, nutrition, reading, and listening to complex music is (Comer & Poussaint, 1992; Tharpe & Gallimore, 1988; Young, 1996).

The naming ceremony marks the transition into life or "new" life. It is the first rite of passage from the unborn to infancy. And as suggested earlier, a naming ceremony is also appropriate when a person has come into a new understanding of his or her life's purpose (Stewart, 1996).

There are many variations on how to select a name and the time in which the ceremony is to be performed. Some traditions hold a naming ceremony within hours of birth, while other traditions will wait a year after birth to name a child. The ceremonies range from the very simple to a series of very elaborate rituals. Equally as diverse is how a name is selected. Some traditions require that the child carries the name of the latest family ancestor of the same sex. Yet in other traditions the child must recognize the name it is given by smiling, by stopping crying, or by sleeping peacefully through the night. If the child does not provide the proper sign, then a new name is selected until the baby does.

Many traditions provide two or more names, one for formal use or in business and the other for family and close friends. This also can include a spiritual name for sacred occasions. One of my "favorite" traditions is where a child does not receive a name until a year after his or her birth - after the village has had the opportunity to observe the child. Then, at each significant transition a new name is added, so that a person's name becomes an account of his or her life.

The Akan of Ghana use the Okra system in the naming of their children. The Okra is a belief that certain characteristics of the Creator are more prominent on certain days than others, and these characteristics will provide some insight to the Creator's intent for one's life (Appendix 4). In recognition of this, a child's name reflects the day on which he or she was born.

Remember Africa is a diverse continent of over 800 different ethnic groups, each having its own way of naming. However, most all recognize that a name is more than a label. In order to be African centered, it is not necessary to follow strictly one tradition, just the essence of what a naming ceremony is. A name should provide understanding about one's life purpose and connect to family traditions. The essence of a naming ceremony is to assign meaning to the initiate and ultimately accountability. Also, it is the ceremony which marks the beginning of the village being responsible for providing the unique needs of the initiate.

My son's naming ceremony incorporated concepts of a family name, multiple names and dedication to the Creator. Once my wife and I learned that "we" were expecting a boy, we agreed that his name would be Lathardus Goggins III in order to carry on a family name. Though his name was picked before he was born, it still needed to be defined. Not just what it is to be a Lathardus Goggins, but specifically what is to be Lathardus Goggins III.

The naming ceremony for my son was held over a weekend two months after his birth. We waited two months primarily because of scheduling conflicts. We invited family and selected friends, including our pastor, to the naming ceremony. These were the people Lathardus Goggins III would first know as his village. A benefit of the two months is it provided us time to "get to know" him better - to see what characteristics or raw talents and energies he possessed. Thus, gaining insight into his potential, to our challenge, and to defining Lathardus Goggins III. A part of that definition is his multiple names: his formal name, Lathardus Goggins III; his spiritual name, Kweku; and his "nickname," Tre. All have implications toward his understanding of who he is.

The following is an outline of the ceremony:

I. Welcome

> Dietra will welcome all to the ceremony and thank all who have participated in/sent gifts to baby shower, etc..

II. Why are we here?

> Lathardus II explains the purpose of ceremony, its importance, and the role of participants.

III. Permission from the Elders to continue.

IV. Libation (recognition of ancestors)

V. Why are naming and expectations important?

> Pastor or spiritual leader

Vi. Expressions/Expectations/Defining what is to be

> Lathardus Goggins III/ Kweku (Wednesday's Child)/Tre
>
> A. Grandparents and Elders
>
> B. Family and Village
>
> C. Parents

VII. Prayer

> Parents hold child between them; grandparents touching the parents; family and godparents touching the grandparents; the rest of village touching the family.

VIII. Presentation (This also included the dedication at church the following day)

During the dedication, the family and congregation read the following litany:

Pastor:	Blessed of the Lord, what do you bring to present to the Lord?
Parents:	We bring with joy our gift of new life.
Pastor:	What are you prepared to do for this child

as demonstration of your gratitude for being entrusted with so great a gift?

Parents: We stand committed to loving each other, to teaching our child to know and reverence God and respect all mankind, and providing support for the development of our child's capacity for self-love and service.

Pastor: Who will covenant with you to assist you in this royal assignment?

Grandparents/Godparents: We do! We pledge ourselves to support in whatever way necessary these parents as they carry out their responsibilities toward this child!

Pastor: Family of God! Will you also covenant to pray for this family?, this child?, for the children of the world?

Congregation: We do!

Pastor: We accept your acknowledgments of gratitude and commitment. We therefore anoint this child, in the name of the Lord Jesus. We shall ask God to bestow wisdom and knowledge upon these guardians of God's gift that through them He might give their child His favor and grace. Let us pray!
....

Please note that this is one example of many possible formats. We embellished the naming ceremony with music (jazz, gospel, traditional West African music), African garb and of course food (Louisiana Gumbo). Someone else would have included drumming or a christening. The important things are that the ceremony helps connect the initiate's name to an understanding of his or her purpose/mission in life, and that the ceremony connects village to the well-being and development of the initiate.

Here are some other activities that will help you construct an African centered, family based, community linked rites of passage process:

Recognizing the ancestors: This can be done by a number of activities such as visiting their graves, telling their stories, perpetuating their skills or hobbies, calling their names during libations or other "significant" moments, so that the ancestral names are familiar, and creating a family tree.

Council of Elders: This can be on three levels: community, family and individual. Community council of elders are those elders that have been recognized by the community for their leadership and wisdom for providing direction. Likewise, family elders provide direction and leadership for a family. An individual's council of elders/ancestors are those elders and ancestors with whom an individual has developed a "kindred spirit", or with whom the individual directly identifies. The council may partly consist of "favorite" historical figures. It is important that some of the persons on the council are living. Through studying the lives and philosophies and through conversations, the council serves as guides and a standard to an individual's thought, behavior and actions. As a Christian, one of the people who sits on my council is Jesus. Others are my late grandfathers and Nat Turner. The living elders on my council are the two or three elders from whom I regularly seek advice and guidance. Not every (living) person on my council knows he or she is on my council. Often, I just show up time to time to "bounce" an idea off him or her, or ask for prayer.

Permission of the Elders: Along with a council of elders comes a concept of asking permission. This is a belief that one should seek permission or guidance from those who have served as philosophical guides and have the most invested in that person's life, those who set the stage for that person to fulfill his or her purpose, before taking action on some significant turning point. Or when speaking in public or a family gathering where one is not an elder, you should seek the permission from that community's elders before you invoke nommo, putting positive or negative energies into the community through the spoken word.

Special Time for Youth to Connect with Elders: It is very important that youth understand that life is a continuum, that one day they will be elders. Also, what two segments are most likely to benefit from one another: the youth needing wisdom and guidance, and elders needing energy and to feel useful. For the very young, this can be something as simple as a day with grandparents once a week or month, or storytime with elders reading books and folktales. For older children and adolescents, volunteering at an elder care facility, participating with elders in some kind of community or creative project, and/or simply checking in with grandparents periodically might be more appropriate.

Discovering and Practicing Family Traditions: This should include doing a family tree to illustrate relationships and the continuity in the family. This activity can include identifying the family griots, the people with all the family stories and the knowledge of how everyone is related, and recording the stories. With this information, a family book can be created and updated. Also, the information can give insight towards the philosophies of the ancestors and what they went through. Other activities can include identifying family heirlooms and lands, forming and participating in family reunions, and creating a family kente design or African-styled family shield (something indicative of African descent).

Visiting Significant African American Historical Sites: Like every culture, African Americans have significant turning points in our history, which must be remembered and revisited in order to learn from the people involved in these events, such as court houses, voter registration sites, sit-ins, where people died, and where communities triumphed. Also, I believe every African American should visit the continent of Africa, particularly west Africa, and communities where strong African traditions have been maintained in the United States, such as Gullah Island off the coast of South Carolina. It should be considered a pilgrimage back home. These activities can be significant in developing a world view, which provides a person with the tools to interpret information from an African center.

Time of Reflection: This can be done through keeping a journal, meditation or prayer. For young children, this can include bedtime prayer or asking them to reflect on the day. What happened? What did you do? As the saying goes, hind sight is 20/20. Thus, some things can be learned through reflection. Therefore, those who reflect have more opportunities to learn. Also, the concept of reflection involves critical thinking. For young initiates, this might include games like memory (match) and chess. While for older initiates this can be done by engaging in activities that seek to: analyze a situation - determine if there is a problem; gather additional useful information; define a specific problem(s); develop a strategy to solve the problem(s); act to solve the problem; evaluate the results of your actions; and if necessary start the process over. Along with critical inquiry, as an advance form of reflection, there is spiritual reflection. As suggested before, Ma'at can be a useful gauge for reflection.

Transition from Youth Groups to Adult Groups: Many churches have some kind of youth or young adult group. These groups should provide preparation for participating in the men's and women's or adult groups. This means youth should have opportunities to practice coordinating a service or an event. When youth meet the requirements for joining the adults' group, a ceremony should be held to mark the transition.

Gardening: This simple activity has embedded within it many lessons, such as: preparing the ground - preparation; sowing seeds - patience; weeding, fertilizing, watering, protection from bugs and other animals - nurture; learning to go through a process - that if you provide good preparation and care, you can expect good results; there are some things beyond your control (weather), but you still do your best and adjust; and being connected to nature (Cosmos) - knowing tomatoes do not just come from the store, but from the earth. And if the things we eat come the earth, then maybe we should not pollute it or our neighborhoods. Also, for many African Americans whose families came from the south, gardening/farming was an important activity. So by maintaining a garden and learning some family stories, the initiates are connecting to their ancestors.

Economic Independence: There is a wide variety of activities which promote economic independence, such as fund raising projects; partnerships with banks to form a "community branch" within the group/class; learning a trade or art skill that can be sold; learning to follow and purchase stocks; connecting an allowance to completing chores and grades, or anything that connects economic reward to effort and completing successfully a project; and identifying what businesses are needed within the African American community and then developing a corresponding business plan. Also, a part of being economically independent is not being bound to greed or to money. Thus, charitable giving (i.e., tithes, offerings, donations, and volunteering) to worthy causes is an important activity towards developing economic independence. Initiates should understand that supporting such activities promotes independence and stability in the community.

Symbols of Transition: Here again there are several possibilities. One symbol of transition that many African Americans can identify with is sitting at the "grown-ups' table" at family meals. Some groups use necklaces or a staff to show progression through the rites of passage process. As an initiate completes a lesson or stage successfully, a bead, cloth or some kind of symbol is added. Some other symbols used to mark transition are the types of dress that are considered to be appropriate. Also, girls being allowed to wear makeup may be used as a symbol of transition. However, guides should know that actions are the most significant symbols. As aforementioned, acting as an adult is the best symbol of being an adult. It should be made clear to the initiates that symbols do not justify the transition. Without completing successfully the preparation, and recognition from the Creator, ancestors, and the elders, the symbol means nothing.

Another activity you can use as a part of an African centered rites of passage process includes learning circles where initiates tutor each other in school work or other learning activities. I have provided the following excerpt

from lesson plans I developed when working with a high
school basketball team:

Lesson 1
I. Opening Ceremony
  A. Everyone yells seven times-Harambee!! - holding
     the last harambee as long as possible. Explain and
     discuss meaning (Let's pull together).

II. Discuss Manhood
  A. Questions: What men do you admire? Why? What
     qualities do you admire? What does it take to be a
     man?

  B. Based on discussion, develop a working definition
     of manhood.

  C. Have students divide into groups and each
     group will name one person from African
     American history that meets definition.

  D. Discussion on qualities of these men.

  E Assignment: Each student is responsible for three
     more names from history.

III. Closing Ceremony
  A. Explain meaning of Pamoja Tuta Shinda
     (Together we will win).

  B. Everyone yells - Pamoja Tuta Shinda

Lesson 2

I. Opening Ceremony

A. Seven Harambees - ask for meaning

II. Brief Discussion on Manhood
   A. Open discussion based on working definition. Refine definition.

III. Formation of "Council of Elders"
   A. Explain Council of Elders. By studying their lives and philosophies, they will serve to provide a standard to judge action and attitudes of the students.

   B. Discuss Nguzo Saba
      1. Pronounce and define each.
      2. Ask students to give examples.

   C. Ask for assignment

   D. Break into groups. Assign each with elders/ancestors to study. Suggest to keep in mind the Nguzo Saba when studying the elders/ancestors.

IV. Closing Ceremony
   A. Everyone yells - Pamoja Tuta Shinda!

Lesson 3

I. Opening Ceremony
   A. Seven Harambees!

II. Brief Discussion of Assigned Elders' Philosophy
   A. Open discussion

III. Form Council of Elders
   A. Select seven elders/ancestors

1. One spot reserved for the coach.
2. Two spots reserved for family or community elder of choice.
3. The team must reach consensus on the rest.

IV. Discuss Common Courtesy
    A. Talk about common courtesy
    B. Assignments:
       1. Study Philosophies of Council.
       2. Use thank-you, welcome, and please.
       3. Compliment a woman /girl daily, in a nonsexual manner; notice the differences.

V. Closing Ceremony
    A. Call and response.

Lesson 4

I. Opening Ceremony
    A. Seven Harambees!

II. Discuss Common Courtesy
    A. How did others respond? How did you feel using common courtesy?

III. Refine Definition of Manhood
    A. Open discussion

IV. Develop Code of Conduct
    A. Based on the definition of manhood, elders' philosophies, and experience with common courtesy, devise basic rules of conduct for the team.

V. Closing Ceremony

    A. Pass out "Lift Every Voice and Sing"
    B. Everyone yells - Pamoja Tuta Shinda

It is important to remember that the aforementioned activities and rituals do not in and of themselves constitute an African centered rites of passage experience. It is when such activities have been orchestrated to: move an initiate to an understanding of his or her life's purpose through the stages of life; prepare an initiate to fulfill this purpose and to accept the responsibility for fulfilling his or her purpose; to provide a safe place to practice the skills needed to fulfill his or her purpose successfully; and to mark clearly the transition between each stage, which constitutes a rites of passage process. This means that the activities that constitute the rites of passage process do not necessarily need to be created by the guides. The guides can utilize other organizations and people to provide educative experiences. However, the guides must maintain control of, responsibility for, and accountability for the overall African centered family-based community-linked rites of passage process.

Final Thoughts

AKO - BEN (War Horn)
A battle cry; A call to action

I hope this discussion has provided you with the necessary information for you to formulate a strategy for an African centered, family based, community linked rites of passage process. I believe that "rites" provides the greatness potential for developing healthy African communities. Through rites, we can ensure that our communities, our elders, our adults and our children are provided the sacred knowledge, experiences and spiritual connections needed for them to fulfill successfully the Creator's intentions for their lives.

Not only does the African centered, family based, community linked rites of passage process transmit collective cultural wisdom, it also provides a philosophical structure which fosters an understanding of one's life as a dynamic, an ongoing transformation to a higher level. So that when "life" brings challenges to an individual or a community, there is an understanding that "this too will pass" - if I/we take the time to learn the lesson that is needed to be learned, I/we can have the faith that I/we will be transformed into a better individual/community.

As a process of learning, the rites of passage process incorporates several factors that learning theorists have considered to be important to cognitive development and academic performance: African centered, family based, community linked rites of passage process provides a cultural/social context by which information and experiences can be interpreted; rites encourages meaning making/generative learning/knowledge construction; rites provides token reinforcement. For completing successfully lessons, rituals, ceremonies, and eventually stages of life, initiates are rewarded with certain symbols and privileges (Ottenberg, 1989); "rites" employs stage growth learning; and rites encourages, what Vygotsky (1962) coined as Zone of Proximal Development (ZPD).

Vygotsky's ZPD and Kenyatta's (1962) observations of the Gikuyu recognized that a child's learning is stifled when the learning experience is not in a social context consistent with the heritage of the child. In order for a student to reach their "highest" potential, they must be coupled with a knowledgeable teacher. By him or her self, a student will learn to the "lower" end of his or her potential. The implication is that a teacher and a student must develop a relationship which nurtures the safety, potential and energy matrix. Furthermore, the relationship between the teacher and student must be based upon the values and symbols agreed upon by the teacher and student. Only through this relationship between those persons seeking knowledge and those who have knowledge can information and experiences be taught, learned, and interpreted at their highest level.

African centered, family based, community linked rites of passage process fosters an understanding that African centered thought and culture are not simply whatever black people "think and do," but are those philosophies and solutions consistent with African themes, symbols and wisdom. By practicing African collective cultural heritage, African communities, families and individuals throughout the diaspora can experience momentum more consistently.

African centered, family based, community linked rites of passage process encourages "us" to start with the end in mind - whatever the village/family is trying to accomplish with the initiate(s). We must provide the context for the initiates to flourish. If we want a healthy, conscious, responsible, contributing adult, we must provide the necessary ingredients (experiences, knowledge, safety) in order for such a person to develop. If a child lives in a world where computer skills are necessary, then he or she should be prepared to use computers. Likewise, if a child is to be an adult, then he or she must be prepared to be an adult.

Without African centered, family based, community

linked rites of passage, families and communities leave the development and useful expression of their members' potential to chance. If a family or community does not provide a rites of passage process, then there cannot be any real expectations for blessings, growth, or advancement. How can you not cultivate your fields and expect a harvest? African American families and communities who do not provide an African centered, family based, community linked rites of passage regulate their members to live life cast in darkness. Members of such families and communities are seriously "at risk" of being unable to see their unique genius or realize their full potential; at risk of being exploited by "others" by having no authentic sense of self, they will cling to others' interpretations of what a person from their background should be doing; at risk of being "retarded", without knowledge of the Creator's intent for their life, they are incapable of intelligence (i.e., the ability to develop a strategy to execute one's purpose); and, ultimately, at risk of being incapable of contributing anything of worth to the "common good" of their family, community, nation, world, and Cosmos.

On the other hand, those who have entered an African centered, family based, community linked rites of passage process will be able to walk in the light of the Creator's intent for their lives. They will be equipped to exercise their intelligence. They will know their village (i.e., unborn, children, adults, elders, ancestors, and the Creator) is operating on their behalf.

Though many people see rites of passage as mystical phenomena, it is a very practical approach to life. The mystical aspect of the African centered rites of passage process is what can be accomplished by someone who has been connected to the Creator, understands what is possible through the guidance of the ancestors and elders, and is committed to make the world a better place for future generations. These are the people who will be a light to the world, and will carry the light into the new day.

For more information on African centered rites of passage, I suggest visiting **The Mawasi Company** website **www.mawasi.com.** There is a growing body of research examining the rites of passage process impact and applicability to education (my area of interest), criminal justice system intervention, prevention of "at risk" behavior, and clinical psychological intervention, just to name a few. By following the rites of passage links, a visitor can get updates on other organizations practicing African centered rites of passage, information on trainers, human development information and the latest books and research on African centered rites of passage.

Appendix 1

Willie Lynch (see note 13) was a British slave owner in the West Indies, probably from Jamaica, who had tried some indoctrination methods to control his Black slaves. He suggested a systematic approach of the age old "divide and conquer" method. He was invited to the colony of Virginia in 1712 to teach these methods to some slave owners in the United States.

This is what Willie Lynch spoke:

"Gentlemen, I greet you here on the bank of the James River in the year of our Lord, 1712. First, I shall thank you, the gentlemen of the colony of Virginia, for bringing me here. I am here to help you solve some of your problems with slaves.

Your invitation reached me on my modest plantation in the West Indies where I have experimented with some of the newest and still the oldest method for control of slaves. Ancient Rome would envy us if my program is implemented.

As our boat sailed south on the James River, named for our illustrious king, whose version of the Bible we cherish, I saw enough to know that your problem is not unique. While Rome used cords of wood as crosses for standing human bodies along its old highways in great numbers, you are here using the tree and the rope on occasion. I caught the whiff of dead slaves hanging from a tree a couple of miles back. You are not only losing valuable stock by hanging, you're having uprisings, slaves are running away, your crops are sometimes left in the fields too long for maximum profit, you suffer occasional fires; your animals are killed.

Gentlemen, you know what your problems are. I do not need to elaborate. I am not here to enumerate your problems. I am here to introduce you to a method of solving them. In my bag here, I have a foolproof method for controlling your Black slaves. I guarantee every one of you that if used correctly, it will control the slaves for at least 300 years. My method is simple, and members of your family or any overseer can use it. I've outlined here a number of differences among the slaves, and I take these differences and make them bigger. I use fear, distrust and envy for control purposes. These methods have worked on my modest plantation in the West Indies, and it will work throughout the South.

Take this simple little list of differences, think about them. On top of my list is age, but it's there only because it starts with an "A". Second is 'Color' or shade! There is intelligence, size, sex, size of plantation, status of plantation, attitude of owner, whether the slaves live in the valley, on a hill, east, west, north, south, has fine or coarse hair, or is tall or short.

Now that you have a list of differences, I shall give you an outline of action, but before I do that, I assure you that the distrust is stronger than trust and envy is stronger than adulation, respect, or admiration. The Black slaves, after receiving the indoctrination, shall carry on and will become self-refueling and self-generating for hundreds of years, maybe thousands.

Don't forget, you must pitch the old Black male versus the young Black male, and the young Black male against the old Black male. You must use the female versus male and male versus female. You must use the dark-skinned slaves versus the light-skinned slaves. You must also have your white servants, overseers distrust all Blacks, but it is necessary that your slaves trust and depend on us. They must love, respect and trust only us.

Gentlemen, the kits are your keys to control. Use them, have your wives and children use them. Never miss opportunities. My plan is guaranteed, and the good thing about this plan is that if used intensely for one year, the

slaves, they will remain perpetually distrustful.
Thank you, gentlemen."

According to Stampp's (1956) **The Peculiar Institution**, control over slaves was best institutionalized when slave masters:

1. Established and maintained strict discipline... It greatly impairs the happiness of a negro, to cultivate an insubordinate temper [think for one's self].
2. Implanted in the [slaves] a consciousness of personal inferiority. They had to know and keep their places, to feel the difference between master and slave, to understand that bondage was their natural status.
3. Trained [school] slaves to be awed with a sense of their master's enormous power. The only principle upon which slavery could be maintained was the power of fear.
4. Persuaded the [slaves] to take an interest in the master's enterprise and to accept his standards of good conduct [values]....... The master should make it his business to show his slaves, that the advancement of his individual interest, is at the same time an advancement of theirs. Once they feel this, it will require but little compulsion to make them act as it becomes them.
5. Impressed Negroes with their helplessness, to create in them a perfect habit of dependence on their masters. Many believed it was dangerous to teach slaves to be skilled artisans in the towns, because they tended to become self-reliant... got a habit of roaming and taking care of themselves....it produces in the slave an unwillingness to return to the regular life and domestic control of the master (pp.144-147).

Appendix 2

Though it may not be necessary to write an essay, it is necessary to examine how you know those for whom you will develop a rites of passage.

Lathardus Goggins III (Tré)
My Symbolic Son: The Packing of a Smile
May 1996

This paper is an attempt to examine how I know my son Tré. He is new to this world, only seven months old. However, I can't imagine my life without him. How did this happen? I struggle to make sense of gestures, babbles, coos and cries. It is almost overwhelming; as soon as I make sense of one, he does something new, or a recently published study challenges the meaning I made. The focus of this paper is Tré's smile; how we (family, friends and acquaintances) "packed" meaning into the smile and respond to the meaning we made, thereby affecting Tré's understanding of himself - the person I am getting to know. I choose a smile because it is the one sign that we use most to gauge Tré's actions and personality.

My first knowing of Tré was Dietra's announcement of "our" being pregnant. Our being pregnant was only in concept. The baby for me was a theoretical concept. Neutral, I had no preference on boy or girl. I could not feel the baby. I only could experience the baby vicariously through Dietra. As my wife shared her experiences with the baby, I was able to draw assumptions. Other people drew assumptions based on the experiences as well: if you are "really sick" at the beginning of the pregnancy means that you're going to have a boy, if baby boys are attracted to you that means that you are having a girl; how you are carrying the baby meant something. The funny thing was for every meaning for "something" we were told, somebody else would provide another interpretation.

My first time "really" knowing Tre` was at five months - the sonagram. We learned that: the baby was a boy; he was healthy; and he was big. Shortly thereafter, his movements became more noticeable. I could see that he was active. I definitely appreciated his activity more than Dietra did. Of course, people had interpretations about things she was feeling: "he's going to be a handful"; "you're having a boy, I feel sorry for you"; "you're lucky, boys are easier to raise than girls."

The first time Dietra and I had to negotiate our interpretations of "baby boy" was in the designing of "Tre`'s room." The room was painted bold forest green, which I thought was fine. Dietra wanted something softer (something babyish). I didn't want anything blue (of course, definitely not pink). Dietra wanted powder blue. I didn't want to perpetuate girl and boy stereotypes. We chose mint green.

Tre` was born October 4, 1995. By this time we had been bombarded with all kinds of interpretations and expectations about what Tre` will be. At 5:00 p.m., Tre` was born, eyes wide open and 8 lbs. Nurses commented that "He is so alert!" Tre` seemed to recognize his parents' voices. Eight pounds meant he was healthy. When he tried to suckle, it meant he "knew" what to do. Then he went to sleep and smiled.

The Smile

There is a saying, "When a baby smiles in his sleep, it means that an angel is whispering in his ear." Of course, we interpreted Tre`'s smiling as a good thing. We would wait for it to happen. At three days old, Tre` began to "half smile" while he was awake, and this was even better than smiling while he was asleep. Smiling while he was awake had to mean he was expressing happiness and contentment.

Next to Tre being alert, the smile is what is commented about the most. Being alert does not necessarily require social interaction. However, a smile is typically associated with a social activity. Therefore, it has been the smile which people have responded to the most.

The smile means happy, or does it? According to a recent study, the smile is linked to activity in the front right quarter of the brain. Initially, a smile is primarily a biological function. Also suggested was the potential for happiness, as indicated by the smile, is biologically influenced. It seems that the smile is a universal human sign to show nonthreatening behavior. For a baby, it means that there is a certain level of comfort and safety. But, how does the baby know this, and what are the effects of this sign of "nonthreatening behavior"?

The Packing of a Smile: "Tre is such a happy baby"

We have assigned values to Tre's smile. These values are assigned based on the experience of the person creating the meaning and the conditions under which Tre smiles. As we (family, friends and associates) share interpretations of the smile, each of us begins to build a multidimensional social construct of Tre. For example, consider the following: When I walk into the same room as Tre, he looks at me and smiles.

My Interpretation
- Tre recognizes me, and is happy to see me.
- He feels protected, loved and comforted.
- His happiness validates my fathering techniques.

Others' Interpretations
- Tré recognizes me, and is happy to see me.
- Tré feels good about "daddy".
- I must spend time with Tré and that time is "good".
- I am a good father.

It is these layers of interpretations that govern our responses to Tré and subsequently his response to "us." To the point which "the smile" becomes much more than a chemical reaction in the front right quarter of the brain and the corresponding muscular twitch, the layers of interpretation surrounding the smile can become so dense and connect to so many other things it begs the question "What came first, the chicken or the egg?" Does Tré respond to our interpretations or do we form interpretations based on Tré's responses? A study of "baby signs" suggests that infants create signs to communicate their ideas long before they talk - a motor skill rather than a cognitive one. However, if the sign does not produce the desired results, the infant will try a new one. Tré has the smile which invites others to interact with him. The interaction provides opportunities for practicing motor, cognitive and social skills. Or does Tré, practicing his cognitive, social and motor skills (the smile), invite us to interact with him? Has Tré molded me into the father I am or have I molded Tré into the son I expected? The truth is both. These interactions also foster the need for expression and self discovery on both our parts.

One of the basic principles of the African centered rites of passage process is that every child has the built in capacity to succeed; that every child has innate characteristics to fulfill his/her life's purpose. Thus, a baby is not an empty concept waiting to be shaped into whatever the environment dictates. However, another principle states that when the village has not provided appropriate content, the child will be "wrecked," suggesting that youth cannot effectively teach themselves to be adults. There is an interplay between what children and adults bring to each situation to foster "proper" development. So we depend on signs to read each other. However, we should be cautious in our reading of each other. I have interpreted Tré's smile as a validation of my fathering techniques. If I allow Tré's smile to be an over determined sign of my "fathering," what kind of father would I be? Are there not times in which being a "good" father requires me to do things that may not bring a smile? Of course.

Tré is a multidimensional, ever-developing person dense with meanings, potential and expectations. I have gotten to know Tré through a dialogue of signs that started with a smile.

Appendix 3
42 Admonitions (Negative Confessions) of Ma'at

One sister suggested that we should not only confess that "I have not ...", but also start each day with "I will not..."

1. I have not done iniquity.
2. I have not robbed with violence.
3. I have not stolen.
4. I have done no murder; I have done no harm.
5. I have not defrauded offerings.
6. I have not diminished obligations.
7. I have not plundered the Netcher. [I have not robbed God].
8. I have not spoken lies.
9. I have not snatched away food.
10. I have not caused pain.
11. I have not committed fornication.
12. I have not caused shedding of tears.
13. I have not dealt deceitfully.
14. I have not transgressed.
15. I have not acted guilefully.
16. I have not laid waste the ploughed land. [I have not polluted the land or wasted natural resources].
17. I have not been an eavesdropper.
18. I have not set my lips in motion (against anyone).
19. I have not been angry and wrathful except for a just cause.
20-21.I have not defiled the wife of any man [or the husband of any woman].
22. I have not polluted myself.
23. I have not caused terror.
24. I have not transgressed.
25. I have not burned with rage.
26. I have not stopped my ears against the words of Right

and Truth (Ma'at).

27. I have not worked grief.
28. I have not acted with insolence.
29. I have not stirred up strife.
30. I have not judged hastily.
31. I have not been an eavesdropper.
32. I have not multiplied words exceedingly.
33. I have not done either harm or ill.
34. I have never cursed the king.
35. I have never fouled the water.
36. I have not spoken scornfully.
37. I have never cursed the Netcher [God].
38. I have not stolen.
39. I have not defrauded the offerings of the Netcher [God].
40. I have not plundered the offerings to the blessed dead.
41. I have not filched the food of the infant, neither have I sinned against the Netcher of my native town. [I have not unjustly willed my power over the weak or sinned against God].
42. I have not slaughtered with evil intent the cattle of the Netcher [God]. [I have not killed God's animals without just cause].

Appendix 4
Akan Spiritual Names

THE SUNDAY CHILD

God Image: **ASI**   Male: **KWESI**   Female: **Esi**

You are born to lead. You have the ability to build support systems, friendships and kinship groups for others. Society looks upon you to lead in bringing people together for the fulfillment of their group goals. In the face of life's accident, you are the guide of the people. In the wilderness you are the haven for the people struggling to find their bearings. You show to friends that you will be there when they need you. People listen to you and care about you because you listen to them, and you care about them. You endorse their uniqueness; you validate them. You realize delay as time-consuming and emotionally demanding: but you are dependable for you and do not let your friends down. There are times when, as a mature person, you may not need friends, and you may be immune to life's accidents; yet friends are essential to you to speak to, to confide in and share your secrets, fears and shame. You can be of immense help to someone who has become dependent on alcohol, drugs, neurotic defenses, and out dated ideologies.

THE MONDAY CHILD

God Image: **ADWO** Male: **KWODWO**   Female: **ADWOA**

You are a peacemaker; unconquerable, full of humor and self-understanding. You are capable of calling out the gifts of qualities of others. You enjoy doing the kind of things that help other people, but you do them also to satisfy yourself. You like trying to help just because you feel you are part of them, and that you do benefit yourself as you help out. You make people feel that they depend upon each other as a corporate social body. The enterprise of your life is to enable people to behave better toward one another. A sense of purpose helps you to feel that you are good. You have a purpose beyond yourself; and this lends a meaning and direction to your existence. Only rarely do you become bored. To you, responsibility to your children and other individuals is a purpose. You are devoted to helping other people despite other claims of your time and energy. You are a friend to the world. While people would say, "This (neighborhood, city, school, church, etc.) is going to the dogs," you say, "It is my responsibility to make it better."

THE TUESDAY CHILD

God Image: **ABE**   Male: **KWABENA**   Female: **ABENA**

You are "mainly" full of fire and determination. You are an inspirator. You are bold. You are a risk taker. What you do is a source of inspiration for others. You do well in works of collective responsibility. You inspire people to do what they need to do. You are willing to risk a change. You can bring about a constructive detour. Certain life crises, managed or accidental, are inevitable for you. You risk letting go of familiar protective identity to stay on a determined purpose. For a while you are exposed and vulnerable; you are forced to live in yourself in a state of uncertainty; yet it is from this that you wet your appetite anew to go through change. Change involves the deepest sort of self-doubt (Often people become too dependent on the institutional parent even to contemplate any risk; and a need for change is often mistranslated). Sometimes only people like you can penetrate the self-doubt - or neutralize negative projections.

You are willing to risk not only losing status or material possession; you are willing to risk losing your life.

THE WEDNESDAY CHILD

God image: **AKU**   MALE: **KWEKU**   Female: **EKUA**

You are a sweet messenger. You have a great capacity for loving. You have the ability to master the environment and engage people in cooperative activities. You possess a sense of confidence; a sense of becoming more independent. You value a strong sense of individual differences and lack animosity in differences among people. You help people support one another in their differences. You can pull people together. You are willing to support your partners in what they want to do for themselves. You do not automatically allow work to take precedence over the people with whom you share their lives. You feel comfortable in revealing yourself to mates or best friends. You can develop multiple success identities. You extricate yourself from personal relationships that become chronologically destructive; you can intuitively pay attention to the needs of the others and their loved ones. Much of what you are known for is your ability to bring the message that is sweet to hear. You bring fame to others.

THE THURSDAY CHILD

God Image: **ADO**   Male: **KWAW**   Female: **ABA**

You are presented with an opportunity to become a transcendent pathfinder. You can go beyond ordinary limits when you are engaged in what you were destined to be involved in. You come to a point where you have to make a decision that invokes sacrificing your comfort for the good of others, even when there is no certainty of return. You engage readily in social and political resistance. You are able to go ahead with what you must be doing, gradually and individually every day, even if it means sitting on an accident waiting for it to happen. Yours is always a courageous act with a religious foundation. The risks you take may not always make you a winner, but you achieve the goals of society even if you merely raise the level of discourse. You make us all more confident in our ability to know what is right. You make people see their collective vocation is to build and develop their community in order to restore people to their traditional greatness. You are a strong one, strong in will power and in political leadership.

THE FRIDAY CHILD

God Image: **AFI**   Male: **KWOFI**   Female: **AFUA**

You are known to be a person full of growth, creativity and ingenuity. You are always anticipating what can be done. You are a wanderer. You have the quality of right timing. As you learn to anticipate the future, you increase your control over the direction of your life. Your primary source of well being is the conviction that your life has meaning and direction. You have the delicate web of love, work, family, purpose and pleasure that might support a fully engaged life, to a considerable degree of right timing. You are capable of training your powers to predict the future. You can search far and find a new dream if you are aware that you are approaching a dead-end. During an accident in your career, you see your new dream. You are adept in anticipation/ imagining future bends in the road and preparing to shift gears in advance. You do realize that the best choice does not always turn out to be the right one, and you have the ability to accept that. (Some people of lower consciousness develop bitterness, which derives from their dwelling on a rational choice that turned out to be wrong). You are a person who sees future possibilities when the road clears, and you see the opening and risk taking it.

THE SATURDAY CHILD

God Image: **AME**   Male: **KWAME**   Female: **AMA**

You are a person of wise and gentle composure, whose gift is for bringing peace to troubled waters. You have reached a clear purpose beyond yourself; and this sustains your well-being. You are the most ancient one. You are the most happy one, full of wisdom. You are the defender of the past. You can be a conduit for spiritual expression. You tend to "rediscover"' faith during a major passage, and you become involved in a major cause. You feel part of a larger intention toward love and justice. You face crisis through prayer. You are reanimated through religion though you are not overly concerned with formal churches.

Calendar # Year of Birth

1   1905, 1911, 1922, 1933, 1939, 1950, 1961, 1967,
     1978, 1989, 1995, 2006, 2017, 2023, 2034, 2045

2   1906, 1917, 1923, 1934, 1945, 1951, 1962, 1979,
     1990, 2001, 2007, 2018, 2035, 2046

3   19 01, 1907, 1918, 1929, 1935, 1946, 1957, 1963,
     1974, 1985, 1991, 2002, 2013, 2019, 2030, 2041

4   1902, 1913, 1919, 1930, 1941, 1947, 1958, 1969,
     1975, 1986, 1997, 2003, 2014, 2025, 2031, 2042

5   1903, 1914, 1925, 1931, 1942, 1953, 1959, 1970,
     1981, 1987, 1998, 2009, 2015, 2026, 2037, 2043

6   1909, 1915, 1926, 1937, 1943, 1954, 1965, 1971,
     1982, 1993, 1999, 2010, 2021, 2027, 2038, 2049

7   1910, 1921, 1927, 1938, 1949, 1955, 1966, 1977,
     1983, 1994, 2005,2011, 2022, 2033, 2039, 2050

8   1900, 1928, 1956, 1984, 2012, 2040

9   1912, 1940, 1968, 1996, 2024

10   1924, 1952, 1980, 2008, 2036

11   1908, 1936, 1964, 1992, 2020, 2048

12   1920, 1948, 1976, 2004, 2032

13   1904, 1932, 1960, 1988, 2016, 2044

14   1916, 1944, 1972, 2000, 2028

Calendar 1

january
sun	mon	tue	wed	thu	fri	sat
1	2	3	4	5	6	7
8	9	10	11	12	13	14
15	16	17	18	19	20	21
22	23	24	25	26	27	28
29	30	31				

february
sun	mon	tue	wed	thu	fri	sat
			1	2	3	4
5	6	7	8	9	10	11
12	13	14	15	16	17	18
19	20	21	22	23	24	25
26	27	28				

march
sun	mon	tue	wed	thu	fri	sat
			1	2	3	4
5	6	7	8	9	10	11
12	13	14	15	16	17	18
19	20	21	22	23	24	25
26	27	28	29	30	31	

april
sun	mon	tue	wed	thu	fri	sat
						1
2	3	4	5	6	7	8
9	10	11	12	13	14	15
16	17	18	19	20	21	22
23	24	25	26	27	28	29
30						

may
sun	mon	tue	wed	thu	fri	sat
	1	2	3	4	5	6
7	8	9	10	11	12	13
14	15	16	17	18	19	20
21	22	23	24	25	26	27
28	29	30	31			

june
sun	mon	tue	wed	thu	fri	sat
				1	2	3
4	5	6	7	8	9	10
11	12	13	14	15	16	17
18	19	20	21	22	23	24
25	26	27	28	29	30	

july
sun	mon	tue	wed	thu	fri	sat
						1
2	3	4	5	6	7	8
9	10	11	12	13	14	15
16	17	18	19	20	21	22
23	24	25	26	27	28	29
30	31					

august
sun	mon	tue	wed	thu	fri	sat
		1	2	3	4	5
6	7	8	9	10	11	12
13	14	15	16	17	18	19
20	21	22	23	24	25	26
27	28	29	30	31		

september
sun	mon	tue	wed	thu	fri	sat
					1	2
3	4	5	6	7	8	9
10	11	12	13	14	15	16
17	18	19	20	21	22	23
24	25	26	27	28	29	30

october
sun	mon	tue	wed	thu	fri	sat
1	2	3	4	5	6	7
8	9	10	11	12	13	14
15	16	17	18	19	20	21
22	23	24	25	26	27	28
29	30	31				

november
sun	mon	tue	wed	thu	fri	sat
			1	2	3	4
5	6	7	8	9	10	11
12	13	14	15	16	17	18
19	20	21	22	23	24	25
26	27	28	29	30		

december
sun	mon	tue	wed	thu	fri	sat
					1	2
3	4	5	6	7	8	9
10	11	12	13	14	15	16
17	18	19	20	21	22	23
24	25	26	27	28	29	30
31						

Calendar 2

january

sun	mon	tue	wed	thu	fri	sat
	1	2	3	4	5	6
7	8	9	10	11	12	13
14	15	16	17	18	19	20
21	22	23	24	25	26	27
28	29	30	31			

february

sun	mon	tue	wed	thu	fri	sat
				1	2	3
4	5	6	7	8	9	10
11	12	13	14	15	16	17
18	19	20	21	22	23	24
25	26	27	28			

march

sun	mon	tue	wed	thu	fri	sat
				1	2	3
4	5	6	7	8	9	10
11	12	13	14	15	16	17
18	19	20	21	22	23	24
25	26	27	28	29	30	31

april

sun	mon	tue	wed	thu	fri	sat
1	2	3	4	5	6	7
8	9	10	11	12	13	14
15	16	17	18	19	20	21
22	23	24	25	26	27	28
29	30					

may

sun	mon	tue	wed	thu	fri	sat
		1	2	3	4	5
6	7	8	9	10	11	12
13	14	15	16	17	18	19
20	21	22	23	24	25	26
27	28	29	30	31		

june

sun	mon	tue	wed	thu	fri	sat
					1	2
3	4	5	6	7	8	9
10	11	12	13	14	15	16
17	18	19	20	21	22	23
24	25	26	27	28	29	30

july

sun	mon	tue	wed	thu	fri	sat
1	2	3	4	5	6	7
8	9	10	11	12	13	14
15	16	17	18	19	20	21
22	23	24	25	26	27	28
29	30	31				

august

sun	mon	tue	wed	thu	fri	sat
			1	2	3	4
5	6	7	8	9	10	11
12	13	14	15	16	17	18
19	20	21	22	23	24	25
26	27	28	29	30	31	

september

sun	mon	tue	wed	thu	fri	sat
						1
2	3	4	5	6	7	8
9	10	11	12	13	14	15
16	17	18	19	20	21	22
23	24	25	26	27	28	29
30						

october

sun	mon	tue	wed	thu	fri	sat
	1	2	3	4	5	6
7	8	9	10	11	12	13
14	15	16	17	18	19	20
21	22	23	24	25	26	27
28	29	30	31			

november

sun	mon	tue	wed	thu	fri	sat
				1	2	3
4	5	6	7	8	9	10
11	12	13	14	15	16	17
18	19	20	21	22	23	24
25	26	27	28	29	30	

december

sun	mon	tue	wed	thu	fri	sat
						1
2	3	4	5	6	7	8
9	10	11	12	13	14	15
16	17	18	19	20	21	22
23	24	25	26	27	28	29
30	31					

Calendar 3

january
sun	mon	tue	wed	thu	fri	sat
			1	2	3	4	5
6	7	8	9	10	11	12
13	14	15	16	17	18	19
20	21	22	23	24	25	26
27	28	29	30	31		

february
sun	mon	tue	wed	thu	fri	sat
					1	2
3	4	5	6	7	8	9
10	11	12	13	14	15	16
17	18	19	20	21	22	23
24	25	26	27	28		

march
sun	mon	tue	wed	thu	fri	sat
					1	2
3	4	5	6	7	8	9
10	11	12	13	14	15	16
17	18	19	20	21	22	23
24	25	26	27	28	29	30
31						

april
sun	mon	tue	wed	thu	fri	sat
	1	2	3	4	5	6
7	8	9	10	11	12	13
14	15	16	17	18	19	20
21	22	23	24	25	26	27
28	29	30				

may
sun	mon	tue	wed	thu	fri	sat
			1	2	3	4
5	6	7	8	9	10	11
12	13	14	15	16	17	18
19	20	21	22	23	24	25
26	27	28	29	30	31	

june
sun	mon	tue	wed	thu	fri	sat
						1
2	3	4	5	6	7	8
9	10	11	12	13	14	15
16	17	18	19	20	21	22
23	24	25	26	27	28	29
30						

july
sun	mon	tue	wed	thu	fri	sat
	1	2	3	4	5	6
7	8	9	10	11	12	13
14	15	16	17	18	19	20
21	22	23	24	25	26	27
28	29	30	31			

august
sun	mon	tue	wed	thu	fri	sat
				1	2	3
4	5	6	7	8	9	10
11	12	13	14	15	16	17
18	19	20	21	22	23	24
25	26	27	28	29	30	31

september
sun	mon	tue	wed	thu	fri	sat
1	2	3	4	5	6	7
8	9	10	11	12	13	14
15	16	17	18	19	20	21
22	23	24	25	26	27	28
29	30					

october
sun	mon	tue	wed	thu	fri	sat
		1	2	3	4	5
6	7	8	9	10	11	12
13	14	15	16	17	18	19
20	21	22	23	24	25	26
27	28	29	30	31		

november
sun	mon	tue	wed	thu	fri	sat
					1	2
3	4	5	6	7	8	9
10	11	12	13	14	15	16
17	18	19	20	21	22	23
24	25	26	27	28	29	30

december
sun	mon	tue	wed	thu	fri	sat
1	2	3	4	5	6	7
8	9	10	11	12	13	14
15	16	17	18	19	20	21
22	23	24	25	26	27	28
29	30	31				

Calendar 4

january

sun	mon	tue	wed	thu	fri	sat
			1	2	3	4
5	6	7	8	9	10	11
12	13	14	15	16	17	18
19	20	21	22	23	24	25
26	27	28	29	30	31	

february

sun	mon	tue	wed	thu	fri	sat
						1
2	3	4	5	6	7	8
9	10	11	12	13	14	15
16	17	18	19	20	21	22
23	24	25	26	27	28	

march

sun	mon	tue	wed	thu	fri	sat
						1
2	3	4	5	6	7	8
9	10	11	12	13	14	15
16	17	18	19	20	21	22
23	24	25	26	27	28	29
30	31					

april

sun	mon	tue	wed	thu	fri	sat
		1	2	3	4	5
6	7	8	9	10	11	12
13	14	15	16	17	18	19
20	21	22	23	24	25	26
27	28	29	30			

may

sun	mon	tue	wed	thu	fri	sat
				1	2	3
4	5	6	7	8	9	10
11	12	13	14	15	16	17
18	19	20	21	22	23	24
25	26	27	28	29	30	31

june

sun	mon	tue	wed	thu	fri	sat
1	2	3	4	5	6	7
8	9	10	11	12	13	14
15	16	17	18	19	20	21
22	23	24	25	26	27	28
29	30					

july

sun	mon	tue	wed	thu	fri	sat
		1	2	3	4	5
6	7	8	9	10	11	12
13	14	15	16	17	18	19
20	21	22	23	24	25	26
27	28	29	30	31		

august

sun	mon	tue	wed	thu	fri	sat
					1	2
3	4	5	6	7	8	9
10	11	12	13	14	15	16
17	18	19	20	21	22	23
24	25	26	27	28	29	30
31						

september

sun	mon	tue	wed	thu	fri	sat
	1	2	3	4	5	6
7	8	9	10	11	12	13
14	15	16	17	18	19	20
21	22	23	24	25	26	27
28	29	30				

october

sun	mon	tue	wed	thu	fri	sat
			1	2	3	4
5	6	7	8	9	10	11
12	13	14	15	16	17	18
19	20	21	22	23	24	25
26	27	28	29	30	31	

november

sun	mon	tue	wed	thu	fri	sat
						1
2	3	4	5	6	7	8
9	10	11	12	13	14	15
16	17	18	19	20	21	22
23	24	25	26	27	28	29
30						

december

sun	mon	tue	wed	thu	fri	sat
	1	2	3	4	5	6
7	8	9	10	11	12	13
14	15	16	17	18	19	20
21	22	23	24	25	26	27
28	29	30	31			

Calendar 5

january
sun	mon	tue	wed	thu	fri	sat
				1	2	3
4	5	6	7	8	9	10
11	12	13	14	15	16	17
18	19	20	21	22	23	24
25	26	27	28	29	30	31

february
sun	mon	tue	wed	thu	fri	sat
1	2	3	4	5	6	7
8	9	10	11	12	13	14
15	16	17	18	19	20	21
22	23	24	25	26	27	28

march
sun	mon	tue	wed	thu	fri	sat
1	2	3	4	5	6	7
8	9	10	11	12	13	14
15	16	17	18	19	20	21
22	23	24	25	26	27	28
29	30	31				

april
sun	mon	tue	wed	thu	fri	sat
			1	2	3	4
5	6	7	8	9	10	11
12	13	14	15	16	17	18
19	20	21	22	23	24	25
26	27	28	29	30		

may
sun	mon	tue	wed	thu	fri	sat
					1	2
3	4	5	6	7	8	9
10	11	12	13	14	15	16
17	18	19	20	21	22	23
24	25	26	27	28	29	30
31						

june
sun	mon	tue	wed	thu	fri	sat
	1	2	3	4	5	6
7	8	9	10	11	12	13
14	15	16	17	18	19	20
21	22	23	24	25	26	27
28	29	30				

july
sun	mon	tue	wed	thu	fri	sat
			1	2	3	4
5	6	7	8	9	10	11
12	13	14	15	16	17	18
19	20	21	22	23	24	25
26	27	28	29	30	31	

august
sun	mon	tue	wed	thu	fri	sat
						1
2	3	4	5	6	7	8
9	10	11	12	13	14	15
16	17	18	19	20	21	22
23	24	25	26	27	28	29
30	31					

september
sun	mon	tue	wed	thu	fri	sat
		1	2	3	4	5
6	7	8	9	10	11	12
13	14	15	16	17	18	19
20	21	22	23	24	25	26
27	28	29	30			

october
sun	mon	tue	wed	thu	fri	sat
				1	2	3
4	5	6	7	8	9	10
11	12	13	14	15	16	17
18	19	20	21	22	23	24
25	26	27	28	29	30	31

november
sun	mon	tue	wed	thu	fri	sat
1	2	3	4	5	6	7
8	9	10	11	12	13	14
15	16	17	18	19	20	21
22	23	24	25	26	27	28
29	30					

december
sun	mon	tue	wed	thu	fri	sat
		1	2	3	4	5
6	7	8	9	10	11	12
13	14	15	16	17	18	19
20	21	22	23	24	25	26
27	28	29	30	31		

Calendar 6

january

sun	mon	tue	wed	thu	fri	sat
					1	2
3	4	5	6	7	8	9
10	11	12	13	14	15	16
17	18	19	20	21	22	23
24	25	26	27	28	29	30
31						

february

sun	mon	tue	wed	thu	fri	sat
	1	2	3	4	5	6
7	8	9	10	11	12	13
14	15	16	17	18	19	20
21	22	23	24	25	26	27
28						

march

sun	mon	tue	wed	thu	fri	sat
	1	2	3	4	5	6
7	8	9	10	11	12	13
14	15	16	17	18	19	20
21	22	23	24	25	26	27
28	29	30	31			

april

sun	mon	tue	wed	thu	fri	sat
				1	2	3
4	5	6	7	8	9	10
11	12	13	14	15	16	17
18	19	20	21	22	23	24
25	26	27	28	29	30	

may

sun	mon	tue	wed	thu	fri	sat
						1
2	3	4	5	6	7	8
9	10	11	12	13	14	15
16	17	18	19	20	21	22
23	24	25	26	27	28	29
30	31					

june

sun	mon	tue	wed	thu	fri	sat
		1	2	3	4	5
6	7	8	9	10	11	12
13	14	15	16	17	18	19
20	21	22	23	24	25	26
27	28	29	30			

july

sun	mon	tue	wed	thu	fri	sat
				1	2	3
4	5	6	7	8	9	10
11	12	13	14	15	16	17
18	19	20	21	22	23	24
25	26	27	28	29	30	31

august

sun	mon	tue	wed	thu	fri	sat
1	2	3	4	5	6	7
8	9	10	11	12	13	14
15	16	17	18	19	20	21
22	23	24	25	26	27	28
29	30	31				

september

sun	mon	tue	wed	thu	fri	sat
			1	2	3	4
5	6	7	8	9	10	11
12	13	14	15	16	17	18
19	20	21	22	23	24	25
26	27	28	29	30		

october

sun	mon	tue	wed	thu	fri	sat
					1	2
3	4	5	6	7	8	9
10	11	12	13	14	15	16
17	18	19	20	21	22	23
24	25	26	27	28	29	30
31						

november

sun	mon	tue	wed	thu	fri	sat
	1	2	3	4	5	6
7	8	9	10	11	12	13
14	15	16	17	18	19	20
21	22	23	24	25	26	27
28	29	30				

december

sun	mon	tue	wed	thu	fri	sat
			1	2	3	4
5	6	7	8	9	10	11
12	13	14	15	16	17	18
19	20	21	22	23	24	25
26	27	28	29	30	31	

Calendar 7

january
sun	mon	tue	wed	thu	fri	sat
						1
2	3	4	5	6	7	8
9	10	11	12	13	14	15
16	17	18	19	20	21	22
23	24	25	26	27	28	29
30	31					

february
sun	mon	tue	wed	thu	fri	sat
		1	2	3	4	5
6	7	8	9	10	11	12
13	14	15	16	17	18	19
20	21	22	23	24	25	26
27	28					

march
sun	mon	tue	wed	thu	fri	sat
		1	2	3	4	5
6	7	8	9	10	11	12
13	14	15	16	17	18	19
20	21	22	23	24	25	26
27	28	29	30	31		

april
sun	mon	tue	wed	thu	fri	sat
					1	2
3	4	5	6	7	8	9
10	11	12	13	14	15	16
17	18	19	20	21	22	23
24	25	26	27	28	29	30

may
sun	mon	tue	wed	thu	fri	sat
1	2	3	4	5	6	7
8	9	10	11	12	13	14
15	16	17	18	19	20	21
22	23	24	25	26	27	28
29	30	31				

june
sun	mon	tue	wed	thu	fri	sat
			1	2	3	4
5	6	7	8	9	10	11
12	13	14	15	16	17	18
19	20	21	22	23	24	25
26	27	28	29	30		

july
sun	mon	tue	wed	thu	fri	sat
					1	2
3	4	5	6	7	8	9
10	11	12	13	14	15	16
17	18	19	20	21	22	23
24	25	26	27	28	29	30
31						

august
sun	mon	tue	wed	thu	fri	sat
	1	2	3	4	5	6
7	8	9	10	11	12	13
14	15	16	17	18	19	20
21	22	23	24	25	26	27
28	29	30	31			

september
sun	mon	tue	wed	thu	fri	sat
				1	2	3
4	5	6	7	8	9	10
11	12	13	14	15	16	17
18	19	20	21	22	23	24
25	26	27	28	29	30	

october
sun	mon	tue	wed	thu	fri	sat
						1
2	3	4	5	6	7	8
9	10	11	12	13	14	15
16	17	18	19	20	21	22
23	24	25	26	27	28	29
30	31					

november
sun	mon	tue	wed	thu	fri	sat
		1	2	3	4	5
6	7	8	9	10	11	12
13	14	15	16	17	18	19
20	21	22	23	24	25	26
27	28	29	30			

december
sun	mon	tue	wed	thu	fri	sat
				1	2	3
4	5	6	7	8	9	10
11	12	13	14	15	16	17
18	19	20	21	22	23	24
25	26	27	28	29	30	31

Calendar 8

january
sun	mon	tue	wed	thu	fri	sat
1	2	3	4	5	6	7
8	9	10	11	12	13	14
15	16	17	18	19	20	21
22	23	24	25	26	27	28
29	30	31				

february
sun	mon	tue	wed	thu	fri	sat
			1	2	3	4
5	6	7	8	9	10	11
12	13	14	15	16	17	18
19	20	21	22	23	24	25
26	27	28	29			

march
sun	mon	tue	wed	thu	fri	sat
				1	2	3
4	5	6	7	8	9	10
11	12	13	14	15	16	17
18	19	20	21	22	23	24
25	26	27	28	29	30	31

april
sun	mon	tue	wed	thu	fri	sat
1	2	3	4	5	6	7
8	9	10	11	12	13	14
15	16	17	18	19	20	21
22	23	24	25	26	27	28
29	30					

may
sun	mon	tue	wed	thu	fri	sat
	1	2	3	4	5	
6	7	8	9	10	11	12
13	14	15	16	17	18	19
20	21	22	23	24	25	26
27	28	29	30	31		

june
sun	mon	tue	wed	thu	fri	sat
					1	2
3	4	5	6	7	8	9
10	11	12	13	14	15	16
17	18	19	20	21	22	23
24	25	26	27	28	29	30

july
sun	mon	tue	wed	thu	fri	sat
1	2	3	4	5	6	7
8	9	10	11	12	13	14
15	16	17	18	19	20	21
22	23	24	25	26	27	28
29	30	31				

august
sun	mon	tue	wed	thu	fri	sat
			1	2	3	4
5	6	7	8	9	10	11
12	13	14	15	16	17	18
19	20	21	22	23	24	25
26	27	28	29	30	31	

september
sun	mon	tue	wed	thu	fri	sat
						1
2	3	4	5	6	7	8
9	10	11	12	13	14	15
16	17	18	19	20	21	22
23	24	25	26	27	28	29
30						

october
sun	mon	tue	wed	thu	fri	sat
	1	2	3	4	5	6
7	8	9	10	11	12	13
14	15	16	17	18	19	20
21	22	23	24	25	26	27
28	29	30	31			

november
sun	mon	tue	wed	thu	fri	sat
				1	2	3
4	5	6	7	8	9	10
11	12	13	14	15	16	17
18	19	20	21	22	23	24
25	26	27	28	29	30	

december
sun	mon	tue	wed	thu	fri	sat
						1
2	3	4	5	6	7	8
9	10	11	12	13	14	15
16	17	18	19	20	21	22
23	24	25	26	27	28	29
30	31					

Calendar 9

january

sun	mon	tue	wed	thu	fri	sat
	1	2	3	4	5	6
7	8	9	10	11	12	13
14	15	16	17	18	19	20
21	22	23	24	25	26	27
28	29	30	31			

february

sun	mon	tue	wed	thu	fri	sat
				1	2	3
4	5	6	7	8	9	10
11	12	13	14	15	16	17
18	19	20	21	22	23	24
25	26	27	28	29		

march

sun	mon	tue	wed	thu	fri	sat
					1	2
3	4	5	6	7	8	9
10	11	12	13	14	15	16
17	18	19	20	21	22	23
24	25	26	27	28	29	30
31						

april

sun	mon	tue	wed	thu	fri	sat
	1	2	3	4	5	6
7	8	9	10	11	12	13
14	15	16	17	18	19	20
21	22	23	24	25	26	27
28	29	30				

may

sun	mon	tue	wed	thu	fri	sat
			1	2	3	4
5	6	7	8	9	10	11
12	13	14	15	16	17	18
19	20	21	22	23	24	25
26	27	28	29	30	31	

june

sun	mon	tue	wed	thu	fri	sat
						1
2	3	4	5	6	7	8
9	10	11	12	13	14	15
16	17	18	19	20	21	22
23	24	25	26	27	28	29
30						

july

sun	mon	tue	wed	thu	fri	sat
	1	2	3	4	5	6
7	8	9	10	11	12	13
14	15	16	17	18	19	20
21	22	23	24	25	26	27
28	29	30	31			

august

sun	mon	tue	wed	thu	fri	sat
				1	2	3
4	5	6	7	8	9	10
11	12	13	14	15	16	17
18	19	20	21	22	23	24
25	26	27	28	29	30	31

september

sun	mon	tue	wed	thu	fri	sat
1	2	3	4	5	6	7
8	9	10	11	12	13	14
15	16	17	18	19	20	21
22	23	24	25	26	27	28
29	30					

october

sun	mon	tue	wed	thu	fri	sat
		1	2	3	4	5
6	7	8	9	10	11	12
13	14	15	16	17	18	19
20	21	22	23	24	25	26
27	28	29	30	31		

november

sun	mon	tue	wed	thu	fri	sat
					1	2
3	4	5	6	7	8	9
10	11	12	13	14	15	16
17	18	19	20	21	22	23
24	25	26	27	28	29	30

december

sun	mon	tue	wed	thu	fri	sat
1	2	3	4	5	6	7
8	9	10	11	12	13	14
15	16	17	18	19	20	21
22	23	24	25	26	27	28
29	30	31				

Calendar 10

january
sun	mon	tue	wed	thu	fri	sat
			1	2	3	4	5
6	7	8	9	10	11	12
13	14	15	16	17	18	19
20	21	22	23	24	25	26
27	28	29	30	31		

february
sun	mon	tue	wed	thu	fri	sat
					1	2
3	4	5	6	7	8	9
10	11	12	13	14	15	16
17	18	19	20	21	22	23
24	25	26	27	28	29	

march
sun	mon	tue	wed	thu	fri	sat
						1
2	3	4	5	6	7	8
9	10	11	12	13	14	15
16	17	18	19	20	21	22
23	24	25	26	27	28	29
30	31					

april
sun	mon	tue	wed	thu	fri	sat
		1	2	3	4	5
6	7	8	9	10	11	12
13	14	15	16	17	18	19
20	21	22	23	24	25	26
27	28	29	30			

may
sun	mon	tue	wed	thu	fri	sat
				1	2	3
4	5	6	7	8	9	10
11	12	13	14	15	16	17
18	19	20	21	22	23	24
25	26	27	28	29	30	31

june
sun	mon	tue	wed	thu	fri	sat
1	2	3	4	5	6	7
8	9	10	11	12	13	14
15	16	17	18	19	20	21
22	23	24	25	26	27	28
29	30					

july
sun	mon	tue	wed	thu	fri	sat
		1	2	3	4	5
6	7	8	9	10	11	12
13	14	15	16	17	18	19
20	21	22	23	24	25	26
27	28	29	30	31		

august
sun	mon	tue	wed	thu	fri	sat
					1	2
3	4	5	6	7	8	9
10	11	12	13	14	15	16
17	18	19	20	21	22	23
24	25	26	27	28	29	30
31						

september
sun	mon	tue	wed	thu	fri	sat
	1	2	3	4	5	6
7	8	9	10	11	12	13
14	15	16	17	18	19	20
21	22	23	24	25	26	27
28	29	30				

october
sun	mon	tue	wed	thu	fri	sat
			1	2	3	4
5	6	7	8	9	10	11
12	13	14	15	16	17	18
19	20	21	22	23	24	25
26	27	28	29	30	31	

november
sun	mon	tue	wed	thu	fri	sat
						1
2	3	4	5	6	7	8
9	10	11	12	13	14	15
16	17	18	19	20	21	22
23	24	25	26	27	28	29
30						

december
sun	mon	tue	wed	thu	fri	sat
	1	2	3	4	5	6
7	8	9	10	11	12	13
14	15	16	17	18	19	20
21	22	23	24	25	26	27
28	29	30	31			

Calendar 11

january

sun	mon	tue	wed	thu	fri	sat
			1	2	3	4
5	6	7	8	9	10	11
12	13	14	15	16	17	18
19	20	21	22	23	24	25
26	27	28	29	30	31	

february

sun	mon	tue	wed	thu	fri	sat
						1
2	3	4	5	6	7	8
9	10	11	12	13	14	15
16	17	18	19	20	21	22
23	24	25	26	27	28	29

march

sun	mon	tue	wed	thu	fri	sat
1	2	3	4	5	6	7
8	9	10	11	12	13	14
15	16	17	18	19	20	21
22	23	24	25	26	27	28
29	30	31				

april

sun	mon	tue	wed	thu	fri	sat
			1	2	3	4
5	6	7	8	9	10	11
12	13	14	15	16	17	18
19	20	21	22	23	24	25
26	27	28	29	30		

may

sun	mon	tue	wed	thu	fri	sat
					1	2
3	4	5	6	7	8	9
10	11	12	13	14	15	16
17	18	19	20	21	22	23
24	25	26	27	28	29	30
31						

june

sun	mon	tue	wed	thu	fri	sat
	1	2	3	4	5	6
7	8	9	10	11	12	13
14	15	16	17	18	19	20
21	22	23	24	25	26	27
28	29	30				

july

sun	mon	tue	wed	thu	fri	sat
			1	2	3	4
5	6	7	8	9	10	11
12	13	14	15	16	17	18
19	20	21	22	23	24	25
26	27	28	29	30	31	

august

sun	mon	tue	wed	thu	fri	sat
						1
2	3	4	5	6	7	8
9	10	11	12	13	14	15
16	17	18	19	20	21	22
23	24	25	26	27	28	29
30	31					

september

sun	mon	tue	wed	thu	fri	sat
		1	2	3	4	5
6	7	8	9	10	11	12
13	14	15	16	17	18	19
20	21	22	23	24	25	26
27	28	29	30			

october

sun	mon	tue	wed	thu	fri	sat
				1	2	3
4	5	6	7	8	9	10
11	12	13	14	15	16	17
18	19	20	21	22	23	24
25	26	27	28	29	30	31

november

sun	mon	tue	wed	thu	fri	sat
1	2	3	4	5	6	7
8	9	10	11	12	13	14
15	16	17	18	19	20	21
22	23	24	25	26	27	28
29	30					

december

sun	mon	tue	wed	thu	fri	sat
		1	2	3	4	5
6	7	8	9	10	11	12
13	14	15	16	17	18	19
20	21	22	23	24	25	26
27	28	29	30	31		

Calendar 12

january

sun	mon	tue	wed	thu	fri	sat
				1	2	3
4	5	6	7	8	9	10
11	12	13	14	15	16	17
18	19	20	21	22	23	24
25	26	27	28	29	30	31

february

sun	mon	tue	wed	thu	fri	sat
1	2	3	4	5	6	7
8	9	10	11	12	13	14
15	16	17	18	19	20	21
22	23	24	25	26	27	28
29						

march

sun	mon	tue	wed	thu	fri	sat
	1	2	3	4	5	6
7	8	9	10	11	12	13
14	15	16	17	18	19	20
21	22	23	24	25	26	27
28	29	30	31			

april

sun	mon	tue	wed	thu	fri	sat
				1	2	3
4	5	6	7	8	9	10
11	12	13	14	15	16	17
18	19	20	21	22	23	24
25	26	27	28	29	30	

may

sun	mon	tue	wed	thu	fri	sat
						1
2	3	4	5	6	7	8
9	10	11	12	13	14	15
16	17	18	19	20	21	22
23	24	25	26	27	28	29
30	31					

june

sun	mon	tue	wed	thu	fri	sat
		1	2	3	4	5
6	7	8	9	10	11	12
13	14	15	16	17	18	19
20	21	22	23	24	25	26
27	28	29	30			

july

sun	mon	tue	wed	thu	fri	sat
				1	2	3
4	5	6	7	8	9	10
11	12	13	14	15	16	17
18	19	20	21	22	23	24
25	26	27	28	29	30	31

august

sun	mon	tue	wed	thu	fri	sat
1	2	3	4	5	6	7
8	9	10	11	12	13	14
15	16	17	18	19	20	21
22	23	24	25	26	27	28
29	30	31				

september

sun	mon	tue	wed	thu	fri	sat
			1	2	3	4
5	6	7	8	9	10	11
12	13	14	15	16	17	18
19	20	21	22	23	24	25
26	27	28	29	30		

october

sun	mon	tue	wed	thu	fri	sat
					1	2
3	4	5	6	7	8	9
10	11	12	13	14	15	16
17	18	19	20	21	22	23
24	25	26	27	28	29	30
31						

november

sun	mon	tue	wed	thu	fri	sat
	1	2	3	4	5	6
7	8	9	10	11	12	13
14	15	16	17	18	19	20
21	22	23	24	25	26	27
28	29	30				

december

sun	mon	tue	wed	thu	fri	sat
			1	2	3	4
5	6	7	8	9	10	11
12	13	14	15	16	17	18
19	20	21	22	23	24	25
26	27	28	29	30	31	

Calendar 13

january

sun	mon	tue	wed	thu	fri	sat
					1	2
3	4	5	6	7	8	9
10	11	12	13	14	15	16
17	18	19	20	21	22	23
24	25	26	27	28	29	30
31						

february

sun	mon	tue	wed	thu	fri	sat
	1	2	3	4	5	6
7	8	9	10	11	12	13
14	15	16	17	18	19	20
21	22	23	24	25	26	27
28	29					

march

sun	mon	tue	wed	thu	fri	sat
		1	2	3	4	5
6	7	8	9	10	11	12
13	14	15	16	17	18	19
20	21	22	23	24	25	26
27	28	29	30	31		

april

sun	mon	tue	wed	thu	fri	sat
					1	2
3	4	5	6	7	8	9
10	11	12	13	14	15	16
17	18	19	20	21	22	23
24	25	26	27	28	29	30

may

sun	mon	tue	wed	thu	fri	sat
1	2	3	4	5	6	7
8	9	10	11	12	13	14
15	16	17	18	19	20	21
22	23	24	25	26	27	28
29	30	31				

june

sun	mon	tue	wed	thu	fri	sat
			1	2	3	4
5	6	7	8	9	10	11
12	13	14	15	16	17	18
19	20	21	22	23	24	25
26	27	28	29	30		

july

sun	mon	tue	wed	thu	fri	sat
					1	2
3	4	5	6	7	8	9
10	11	12	13	14	15	16
17	18	19	20	21	22	23
24	25	26	27	28	29	30
31						

august

sun	mon	tue	wed	thu	fri	sat
	1	2	3	4	5	6
7	8	9	10	11	12	13
14	15	16	17	18	19	20
21	22	23	24	25	26	27
28	29	30	31			

september

sun	mon	tue	wed	thu	fri	sat
				1	2	3
4	5	6	7	8	9	10
11	12	13	14	15	16	17
18	19	20	21	22	23	24
25	26	27	28	29	30	

october

sun	mon	tue	wed	thu	fri	sat
						1
2	3	4	5	6	7	8
9	10	11	12	13	14	15
16	17	18	19	20	21	22
23	24	25	26	27	28	29
30	31					

november

sun	mon	tue	wed	thu	fri	sat
		1	2	3	4	5
6	7	8	9	10	11	12
13	14	15	16	17	18	19
20	21	22	23	24	25	26
27	28	29	30			

december

sun	mon	tue	wed	thu	fri	sat
				1	2	3
4	5	6	7	8	9	10
11	12	13	14	15	16	17
18	19	20	21	22	23	24
25	26	27	28	29	30	31

Calendar 14

january
sun	mon	tue	wed	thu	fri	sat
						1
2	3	4	5	6	7	8
9	10	11	12	13	14	15
16	17	18	19	20	21	22
23	24	25	26	27	28	29
30	31					

february
sun	mon	tue	wed	thu	fri	sat
		1	2	3	4	5
6	7	8	9	10	11	12
13	14	15	16	17	18	19
20	21	22	23	24	25	26
27	28	29				

march
sun	mon	tue	wed	thu	fri	sat
		1	2	3	4
5	6	7	8	9	10	11
12	13	14	15	16	17	18
19	20	21	22	23	24	25
26	27	28	29	30	31	

april
sun	mon	tue	wed	thu	fri	sat
						1
2	3	4	5	6	7	8
9	10	11	12	13	14	15
16	17	18	19	20	21	22
23	24	25	26	27	28	29
30						

may
sun	mon	tue	wed	thu	fri	sat
	1	2	3	4	5	6
7	8	9	10	11	12	13
14	15	16	17	18	19	20
21	22	23	24	25	26	27
28	29	30	31			

june
sun	mon	tue	wed	thu	fri	sat
				1	2	3
4	5	6	7	8	9	10
11	12	13	14	15	16	17
18	19	20	21	22	23	24
25	26	27	28	29	30	

july
sun	mon	tue	wed	thu	fri	sat
						1
2	3	4	5	6	7	8
9	10	11	12	13	14	15
16	17	18	19	20	21	22
23	24	25	26	27	28	29
30	31					

august
sun	mon	tue	wed	thu	fri	sat
		1	2	3	4	5
6	7	8	9	10	11	12
13	14	15	16	17	18	19
20	21	22	23	24	25	26
27	28	29	30	31		

september
sun	mon	tue	wed	thu	fri	sat
					1	2
3	4	5	6	7	8	9
10	11	12	13	14	15	16
17	18	19	20	21	22	23
24	25	26	27	28	29	30

october
sun	mon	tue	wed	thu	fri	sat
1	2	3	4	5	6	7
8	9	10	11	12	13	14
15	16	17	18	19	20	21
22	23	24	25	26	27	28
29	30	31				

november
sun	mon	tue	wed	thu	fri	sat
			1	2	3	4
5	6	7	8	9	10	11
12	13	14	15	16	17	18
19	20	21	22	23	24	25
26	27	28	29	30		

december
sun	mon	tue	wed	thu	fri	sat
					1	2
3	4	5	6	7	8	9
10	11	12	13	14	15	16
17	18	19	20	21	22	23
24	25	26	27	28	29	30
31						

Notes

1. Refers to the person in the rites of passage process who has not yet become a member of the next stage.

2. Kenneth Stampp (1956), Frederick Douglass (1845/ 1968), Horace M. Bond (1966), Carter G. Woodson (1933/1990) are some of the scholars who have discussed the dehumanization and oppression of African Americans. This process often included separating tribes and families. Also, Africans were split along many social lines to ensure that forming community and the transmission of cultural heritage were most difficult (see Appendix 1).

3. Carl Rogers (1951) defined the configuration of self as being "composed of such elements as the perceptions of one's characteristics and abilities; the percepts and concepts of self in relation to others and to the environment; the value qualities which are perceived as associated with experiences and objects; and goals and ideas which are perceived as having positive or negative valence" (pp. 136 - 137).

4. Most people assume that evolution and creation are opposite. However, few have discussed the possibility of the two concepts being complementary. One of my college chemistry professors suggested that science can never answer the question "why?". Science can discover what, when, how, but never why. When people look closely at the theory of evolution and verses on creation (Genesis 1), they tend to support one another in where life began, how life progressed from plants to animals, and from starting in the seas and moving onto land.

5. The equation for gravitational force (attraction) is:

$$F = \frac{GM_1M_2}{R^2}$$

where F is the gravitational force; G is the constant .0000000667; M1 is the mass of one object; M2 is the mass of the second object; and R is distance between the two objects. This equation never equals zero. Therefore, there is always an attraction between any object and any other object in universe or the universe itself. Subsequently, if your mass ceases to exist, the whole universe would have to shift to compensate.

6. However, it is never too late to correct what went wrong. This is the essence of sankofa and repentance.

7. What I can say? Carter G. Woodson's famous quote is appropriate: "If you can control a man's thinking, you do not have to worry about his action. When you determine what a man shall think, you do not have to concern yourself with what he will do. If you make a man feel that he is inferior, you do not have to compel him to accept an inferior status, for he will seek it himself. If you make a man think that he is justly an outcast, you do not have to order him to the back door. He will go without being told; and if there is no back door, his very nature will demand one." Those whose minds are infected with white European male supremacy will perpetuate it through actions, speech and images even when the facts suggest something different (Daniel 7:6 and Revelation 1: 14 & 15). Many of those who have false images of Jesus argue that the color of Jesus is insignificant to Christianity. I would agree that what Jesus looks like is "truly" insignificant to the Christian philosophy. However, if

the color of Jesus is not important then why be so emotionally attached to a lie?

8. Another extension of accepting mainstream's perceptions becoming the reality of African American youth is the belief that sports offer the only way to success, particularly basketball. When polled, 78% of African American male high school students said they believe that they could make it to the NBA. The reality is 1 out of 10,000.

9. Self efficacy is how capable someone judges him or herself to be in a given situation. It is a person's sense of "I can do it."

10. Closely looking at Africa, one sees many contradictions to the philosophy of communalism and harmony. Please consider that philosophy and practice are not the same. Much like loving one's enemy is part of the Christian philosophy, but it is not "always" practiced. Another issue is that many historical solutions between various people have been nullified because of the Berlin conference. When American and European leaders arbitrarily divided African into countries with little to no consideration of cultural and social boundaries, they forced together groups that had historically avoided one another.

11. Much of the research concerning African Americans uses a deficiency analysis; subsequently, the solutions tend to suggest a need for compensation programs designed to align African American student learning styles and values with the mainstream. This deficiency analysis has led to the general

characterization of people of African descent as "disadvantaged," "culturally deprived," "dysfunctional," "at risk," permanent underclass, and other nomenclature derived from a deficiency analysis (e.g., ADD and learning disabled). The phenomenon of viewing others as deficient is also perpetuated within families. It happens when a child is called "bad." Nommo suggests that when a bad child acts bad, it should be expected. However, when a "good" child acts bad, then there was a problem.

12.   Barbarians is the term used by the Romans to refer to the tribes of northern Europe such as the Angles, Saxons, and Franks.

13.   Though the historical validity of this speech is seriously questioned, it is representative of strategies used to "divide" us not only from one another, but from our means of transmitting collective cultural wisdom.

References

Ani, M. (1994). Yurugu: An African centered critique of European cultural thought and behavior. Trenton, NJ: Africa World Press.

Asante, M. K. (1987). The Afrocentric idea. Philadelphia: Temple Press.

Bandura, A. (1977). Social learning theory. Englewood Cliffs, NJ: Prentice-Hall.

Bandura, A. (1986). Social foundations of thought and action: A social cognitive theory. Englewood Cliffs, NJ: Prentice-Hall.

Biko, S. (1978). I write what I like. New York: Harper & Row.

Bond, H. M. (1966). The education of the Negro in the American social order. New York: Octagon Books.

Boykin, A. W. (1986). The triple quandary and the Afro-American children. In U. Neisser (Ed.), The school achievement of minority children, (pp. 57-92). Hillsdale, NJ: Lawrence Erlbaum Assoc.

Childs, F. (1997, May). Keynote speaker at D. Moss (chair), Liela Green Alliance of Black School Educators Conference: Canton, OH.

Comer, J. P. & Poussaint, A. F. (1992). Raising Black children. New York: Plume.

Cross Jr., W. E., Parham, T. A. & Helms, J. E. (1991). The stages of black identity development: Nigrescence models. In R. L. Jones (Ed.), Black psychology, 3rd ed, (pp. 319-338). Berkeley, CA: Cobb & Henry Publishers.

Dewey, J. (1938/1963). Experience & education. New York: Collier Books.

Douglass, F. (1845/1968). Narrative of the life of Frederick Douglass: Am American slave. New York: Signet.

Erikson, E. H. (1982). The life cycle completed: A review. New York: Norton.

Evans, T. (1993, February). Black men: Toward a brighter future. In A. Kambon (Chair), Black Men: Harambee! Columbus, OH.

Felder, C. H. (Ed.) (1993). Original African heritage study Bible. Nashville: The James S. Winston Publishing.

Frankl, V. (1962). Man's search for meaning. Boston: Beacon Press.

Freire, P. (1970). Pedagogy of the oppressed. New York: The Continuum Publishing.

Freud, S. (1933). New introductory lectures on psycho-analysis. (W. J. H. Sprott, Trans.). New York: W. W. Norton.

Goggins II, L. (1996). African centered rites of passage and education. Chicago: African American Images.

Hill Jr., P. (1992). Coming of age: African American male rites of passage. Chicago: African American Images.

Irvine, J. J. (1991). Black students and school failure. New York: Praeger Publishers.

Johnson, R. (1996). Boys and fatherhood. In Fathers, Families and Communities. Sacramento, CA.

Karenga, M. (1994). Introduction to Black studies. Los Angeles: The University of Sankore Press.

Kenyatta, J. (1962). Facing Mount Kenya. New York: Vintage Books.

Khalifah, H. K. (1993). The campaign of Nat Turner: The complete text of the confessions of the leader of the most successful slave revolt the United States history. Newsport News, VA: U.B. & U.S. Communications Systems.

Kunjufu, J. (1985). Countering the conspiracy to destroy Black boys. Chicago: African American Images.

Maquet, J. (1967/1972). Africanity. (Joan R. Rayfield, Trans.). New York: Oxford University Press.

M.E.C.C.A. (n.d.). African Americans resurrect rites of passage through a comprehensive family & community development model.

Mensah, A. (1991). Preliminary materials for the development of a rites of passage course. Milwaukee, WI: Mensah Publications.

Munroe, M. (1992). In pursuit of purpose. Shippensburg, PA: Destiny Images Publishers.

Nash, J. M. (1997). Fertile minds, Time, February 3, pp. 48-56.

Ottenberg, S. (1989). Boyhood rituals in a African society: An interpretation. Seattle: University of Washington Press.

P540 Bandura Group (1996). Overview of Bandura's theory: Social learning theory. Available: http://education.indiana.edu/cep/courses/p540/bandsc.html.

Patton, J. M. (1993). Psychological assessment of gifted and talented African American. In J. H. Stanfield & D. H. Rutledge (Eds.), Race and ethnicity in research methods. (pp. 198-216). Newbury Park, CA: Sage Publications.

Perkins, U. E. (1986). Harvesting new generations: The positive development of Black youth. Chicago: Third World Press.

Peters, J. (1997, August 10). Watch and be ready! In the Arlington Church of God 11:00 service (Ronald J. Fowler, pastor). Akron, OH.

Piaget, J. (1954). The construction of reality for the child. New York: Basic Books.

Rogers, C. R. (1951). Client-centered therapy: Its current practice implications, and theory. Boston: Houghton Mifflin Company.

Shade, B. (1989). Cognitive style, what is it? Afro-American cognitive patterns. In B. Shade (Ed.) Culture, style and the educative process. (pp. 87-115). Springfield, IL: Charles C. Thomas Publisher.

Shaffer, D. (1993). Developmental psychology. Pacific Grove, CA: Brooks/Cole.

Skinner, B. F. (1953). Science and human behavior. New York: McMillian.

Some, M. (1993). Ritual: Power, healing and community. Portland, OR:Swan/Raven & Company.

Some, M. (1994). Rites of passage. Utne Reader, 64, 67-68.

Stampp, K. M. (1956). The peculiar institution. New York: Alfred A. Knopf.

Stewart, J. (1996). 1,001 American names:First and last names from the African continent. Secaucus, NJ: Citadel Press.

Tedla, E. (1996). Sankofa: African thought and education. New York: Peter Lang

Tharpe, R. G. & Gallimore, R. (1988). Rousing minds to life. Cambridge, MA: Cambridge University Press.

Vygotsky, L. (1962). Thought and language. Cambridge, MA: MIT Press

Wiley, R. (1994). What Black people should do now: Dispatches from near the vanguard. New York: Ballantine Books.

Woodson, C. G. (1933/1990). The mis-education of the Negro. Trenton, NJ: Africa World Press, Inc..

Wright, D. (1997, Spring Semester). Lecture, In Higher Education Curriculum and Program Planning (Dianne Brown-Wright, instructor). The University of Akron.

Young, M. E. (1996). Early child development: Investing in the future. Washington D.C.: The World Bank.

Permission Credits

Kenyatta, J. (1962). Facing Mount Kenya. New York: Vintage Books. Printed with permission from Random House.

Some, M. (1993). Ritual: Power, healing and community. Portland, OR:Swan/Raven & Company. pp. 66-69. Printed with permission from Penguin Putnam.

Stampp, K. M. (1956). The peculiar institution. New York: Alfred A. Knopf. pp. 144-147. Printed with permission from Random House.

About the Author

Lathardus Goggins II has been a social and community activist for more than fifteen years. He has supported and organized a variety of community-based groups and events. Goggins has earned a Bachelor of Arts degree in Geography and a Master of Education degree in Cultural Foundations of Education. Goggins also holds certificates in AIDS/HIV prevention for African Americans, African American Studies, and African Rites of Passage Facilitation and Instruction. He has also traveled extensively throughout the United States, Canada, The Netherlands, Australia, Mexico, Panama, The Virgin Islands, Puerto Rico, and Africa in the countries of Senegal, Benin, Cote d'Ivoire, Nigeria, Tanzania, Kenya and Ethiopia.

Goggins has made numerous presentations on a variety of subjects, including: Developing Consciousness; Manhood from a Black Consciousness Perspective; Operating in Cultural Diversity; African Centered Rites of Passage as a Factor for Positive Academic Success; and Family-Based Community-linked African Centered Rites of Passage. If you are interested in having Lathardus Goggins II facilitate a workshop or to speak to your group, contact The Mawasi Company at www.mawasi.com or P.O. Box 1852 Akron, OH 44309.

African Centered Rites of Passage and Education

This book provides a clear and thought provoking discussion about an effective solution to many of the basic problems facing African American students. Goggins examines the relationship between African centered rites of passage and the education processes. The following questions frame the discussion: How is sense of self dealt within rites of passage, and specifically within African Centered Rites of Passage? What is the theory regarding the construction of self and its relationship to the educative experience? What are the operating assumptions about "educating" African Americans? and In what ways does the rites of passage process influence the educative experience? The analysis is drawn from an extensive literature review of noted scholars and narratives from people involved in the rites process. Goggins discusses the educative process, formation of purpose and discipline, and the tragedy of parental and community "noninvolvement" in educating African American students. African Centered Rites of Passage and Education is a must read for parents, educators, scholars, students, pastors and all who are concerned about the education of African American students.

African Centered Rites of Passage and Education and other publications are available at **Resource Books** on **www.mawasi.com.**